AN ANTHOLOGY OF BELIZEAN LITERATURE

English, Creole, Spanish, Garifuna

I0592437

Edited by
Víctor Manuel Durán

University Press of America,® Inc.
Lanham · Boulder · New York · Toronto · Plymouth, UK

Copyright © 2007 by
University Press of America,® Inc.
4501 Forbes Boulevard
Suite 200
Lanham, Maryland 20706
UPA Acquisitions Department (301) 459-3366

Estover Road
Plymouth PL6 7PY
United Kingdom

All rights reserved
Printed in the United States of America
British Library Cataloging in Publication Information Available

Library of Congress Control Number: 2006941023
ISBN-13: 978-0-7618-3725-1 (clothbound : alk. paper)
ISBN-10: 0-7618-3725-6 (clothbound : alk. paper)
ISBN-13: 978-0-7618-3724-4 (paperback : alk. paper)
ISBN-10: 0-7618-3724-8 (paperback : alk. paper)

♾™ The paper used in this publication meets the minimum
requirements of American National Standard for Information
Sciences—Permanence of Paper for Printed Library Materials,
ANSI Z39.48—1984

For all Belizean authors, past and present, who through their writings have made us proud to be Belizeans.

For my mother, Emilia Olivera, whose nighttime stories as I was growing up in Progreso instilled in me a love of literature.

For my siblings, Lucila Fredewinda, Virgilia Victoria, Ramiro Nicandro, Juana Isabel, Erasmo John, Edita Irene, and the late Sergia María who have always led by example.

For Adela and all my children, a constant source of inspiration and support.

A special thanks to Mrs. Cindy Sparling for her invaluable help in getting this manuscript ready.

My sincerest gratitude to Dr. Suzanne Ozment, Executive Vice Chancellor for Academic Affairs, University of South Carolina Aiken, without whose support this project would not have materialized.

CONTENTS

PREFACE

There is no doubt that the literature of Belize is currently undergoing a metamorphosis in its content and focus as well as in its universal popularity and serious literary appeal. Belizean literature is expressed through many literary genres and in many of our different and culturally wealthy languages and dialects. The literature of Belize succeeds, in the   opinion of this writer, in expressing the ambitions, hopes, desires, dreams, aspirations, myths and frustrations of the people of this tiny Central American country as they struggle to understand their past, strive to unravel their multifaceted identity and attempt, through an understanding of who they are, to be proud of their polifaceted historical, cultural, social and racial heritage. The literature of Belize is unique because the country itself is unique: gem-like in its natural beauty and appearance, this country stands out in Central America because it is the only one in all of Latin America that has English as its official language, yet strongly manifests itself politically because of its long tradition of democracy (with the exception of Costa Rica, almost unique in this endeavor), linguistically because of the many languages and dialects spoken in this country and socially, not only because all Belizeans are bilingual or trilingual but also because of the racial harmony that exists between members of different ethnic groups, all proudly coexisting and living together, first and foremost, as Belizeans.

Growing up and attaining my fundamental and therefore basic academic formation in the north of Belize, I was always interested in and magnetically drawn to the study of the local myths and legends as expressed in the contemporary oral tradition by my ancestors and their friends. One of the most vivid and pleasurable memories I have is that of my mother turning the kerosene lights off to conserve energy at dusk and hearing her voice in the dark as she related to us stories, legends and myths which she had heard from her own parents and friends as she was growing up. It is these mythical stories that helped spark my interest in literature as an expression of the passions, the myths, the frustrations and the will of the people from which it springs.

The anthology that follows is I think the first of its kind in that it compiles Belizean literature in all literary genres and in all languages and dialects in which it was and is written. It is an attempt to comprehensively compile selected portions of our writings in one book so that in one reading the public will have more than a passing knowledge and more than a superficial awareness of what comprises the literature of Belize. It is my sincerest desire that this anthology serves this purpose.

Víctor Manuel Durán
Aiken, South Carolina
July 10, 2006

ACKNOWLEDGEMENTS

Copyright Raymond Barrow, Mary Gómez Parham, Colville S. Young, Evadne Garcia, E. Roy Cayetano, George C. Price, David Ruiz Puga, Edison Coleman, Philip Lewis, Glenn Godfrey, Evan X. Hyde, J. Alexander Bennett, Byron Foster, Zoila Ellis, Jessie Nunez Castillo, Milton Arana, Cubola Proeuctions.

The editor has made every effort to trace copyright holders, but in a few cases without success. The editor will be very glad to hear from anyone who has been inadvertently overlooked and make the necessary changes at the very first opportunity.

INTRODUCTION

With a population of just above two hundred thousand, the country of Belize, located south of Mexico, has a highly amorphous racial mixture underpinned by a history that is picturesque, varied and textually wealthy. Although most Belizeans claim a mixed ancestry, the main ethnic divisions are the Mayas, the Creoles, the Garifuna (Garinagu), the Mestizos and small pockets of Spanish and English Europeans, African, Chinese, East Indians and Arabs, each group with its own language, customs and traditions, yet each co-existing peacefully and unified, generally, by the Spanish and English languages and by the proud claim of all being Belizeans.

The documented history of the Mayas of Belize contends that this people have been in the country since 2,500 B.C. History tells us that the Mayas, a highly advanced tribe by all measurable standards, reached their cultural and intellectual apex between the seventh and ninth centuries. The Mayas were expert farmers who utilized advanced methods of agriculture such as drainage canals and raised and terraced fields for a more productive cultivation of their agricultural products. They studied astronomy, invented an accurate calendar, used mathematics based on the concept of zero, built magnificent temples that are still standing today and that are represented in the North of Belize by Lamanai and Altun Ha and in the West by Xunantunich and the newly discovered Caracol. From the early sixteenth century to the eighteenth century, political domination of Belize fluctuated between the Mayas and the Spaniards. For example, an expedition led by the Spaniard, Dávila, in the sixteenth century was quelled by Nachankan a Maya Chieftan, with the help of a Spaniard, Gonzalo Guerrero, who had married the chief's daughter. Guerrero is known today as the father of the Mestizo race. British domination and territorial claim of Belize was initiated by Bartholomew Sharpie, an ex-buccaneer now logwood[1] cutter, who led the "invasion" of British settlers intent on exploiting the logwood. Later, the British settlers moved into the interior of Belize, seeking to exploit Belizean hardwoods such as mahogany, sapodilla and Santa María. The Belize Mayas resisted the invasion and occupation of their territory and in 1788 attacked the British woodcutters around the New River in the north of the country. However, despite strong resistance, the Mayas were forced back into the interior of the country in 1802 and some of them settled around the town of San Ignacio in the western portion of Belize. The last Maya resistance of the British occurred in 1872 when, in the town of Orange Walk in the north, the Maya leader, Marcus Canul, attacked the British barracks, demanding rent and land. Tragically, Marcus Canul and his followers were unable to capture the barracks and he was killed by the British.

In Belize, the Mayas are divided into the Mopan, Kekchi and the Yucatec and together form about eleven percent of the total population. The Mopan Mayas got their name from the Mopan River in the west around which they live; they settled, since the early nineteenth century, in the southern district called Toledo and in the west in the Cayo District, after fleeing from forced labor, military conscription and heavy taxes in Guatemala. The Kekchi Mayas live in small communities around San Antonio in the south. Most of the Kekchis came to Belize about 1884, as refugees from the Vera Paz area of Guatemala. They are subsistence farmers, cultivating corn, beans, rice and raising pigs as a meat supplement to their diet. They speak their own Maya dialect and still practice their own ancient rituals, particularly in such areas of marriage and religion. It is interesting to note that their ancient practices and beliefs are conducted alongside Christian practices. This syncretism of religious practices seems to be common in Latin American countries with large indigenous populations such as Mexico, Guatemala and the countries of the Andean regions in South America. The Yucatec Mayas were refugees who immigrated from Yucatan, Mexico, in the time of the Caste War in the late nineteenth century. This Mayan tribe live primarily in the north of Belize and out of the three Mayan groups are the most "hispanicized" since they speak mostly Spanish and are mostly Catholic.

The Creoles comprise about thirty percent of the total population and are direct descendants of the African slaves brought by the British to work in the mahogany and logwood industries. In many cases the slave masters, usually of English or Scot origin, mixed with the African women and produced different racial shades of Creoles. The Creoles live primarily in the city of Belize and still maintain their culture, customs and traditions which to a great extent can be traced to their African heritage. Among their most popular tradition is the Anancy[2] story which has its origins in the Anancy of the Ashanti tribe of African folklore.

The Garifunas comprise about seven percent of the total population of Belize. This tribe formerly known as Black Carib Indians, also inhabits parts of the Atlantic coast of Guatemala, Honduras and Nicaragua. The Garifunas descended from the Island Caribs of Saint Vincent in the eastern Caribbean who had intermarried with escaped African slaves in about 1765. A fierce warrior tribe, the Caribs of St. Vincent first struggled against the Spaniards, then against the French and later against the British to keep themselves from being enslaved. Finally, after several battles, they were captured by the British in 1798 who banished about four thousand of them to the shores of Central America from where they migrated quickly to the mainland. They first appeared in Belize as a group about 1802 and formed villages along the southern coast of the country. The British settlers who populated this area were fearful of this independent, fierce and free group of blacks and did their best to turn their own slaves against them by labeling them as "devil worshippers" and propagating undocumented stories that depicted the Caribs as cannibals and witch doctors. After the 1832 revolution in Honduras, a large number of Garifunas fled that country and landed in Belize, thus swelling the number of Garifunas already inhabiting the southern coast of this country.

The term Mestizos refers to the racial mixture of Spanish and Maya and the first Mestizos who settled in the north of Belize, in the towns of Corozal and Orange Walk, around 1850 were refugees of the Caste War of Yucatan. Later they were joined by many Maya immigrants and expanded their settlements into the islands of Caye Caulker and Ambergris Caye. The Mestizos who came to the North of Belize were Spanish-speaking and Catholic, and, joined later by other Mestizos who came as refugees from other Central American countries, form forty three percent of the total population of Belize. The Mestizo population dominates the culture and traditions of Belize, particularly in areas of religion, the Spanish language and family life. Mestizos are fiercely Catholic and culturally unique in their regard for close family ties with very strict rules of courtship and marriage. Mestizo food, based on corn and its byproducts, is a mixture of Spanish and Maya cuisine and is tremendously popular throughout the country. Like the Garifuna, the Mestizos are fiercely proud of their traditions, customs and culture and propagate them through their literature and legends which they disseminate both orally and in writing.

This amalgam of different ethnic groups forms the core of the population of Belize. As noted in the preface, one of the common bonds of this multicultural and multiracial group is that all the different ethnic groups consider themselves Belizeans, first and foremost. As a cohesive group of Belizeans, the culturally and linguistically diverse ethnic entities joined together in a peaceful, progressive and joyous "revolution" led, in the late fifties and early sixties, by a proud Belizean native, George C. Price, to achieve, *peacefully*, the political independence of Belize from Great Britain on September 21, 1981. George Cadle Price, the "father of Belize independence" then became the first Prime Minister of Belize and is today a much respected person in the political history of the country of Belize.

As specified earlier, when the Mestizos and Mayas came to the north of Belize, their language was Spanish-therefore the history of the literature of Belize is reflected and expressed in the languages of Spanish, Creole, Garifuna and English and this anthology of Belizean Literature will be from writings in these languages.

Because an anthology of this nature has not been heretofore seriously attempted, then the question as to what comprises Belize literature arises. Should Belizean literature embrace writings about Belize written *only* by native Belizeans, naturalized or not, or should Belizean literature comprise solely of literature about Belize written *both* by Belizeans and by non-Belizeans? In this anthology, the editor has made a conscious and hopefully popular choice to include only literature of all genres written about Belize by native and naturalized Belizeans with the hope that other anthologies may be compiled to include all writings about Belize by all writers, native and non-native.

The second question that arises in such an innovative anthology has to do with the literary option of choosing either a chronological or a thematic approach to such a unique collection. Because of the multilingual nature of the documented writings about Belize by Belizeans it is highly impractical to utilize a strictly chronological approach since the authors write about events in their history which may have happened simultaneously with other events that occur in other ethnic tribes in the same country. Thus, for example, the Garifunas in the south may write about a historical occurrence in their chronology that occurred at the same time that another historical occurrence was taking place for the "hispanicized" Mayas in the north. This anthology will therefore utilize a literary and critical approach that can be classified as thematic: that is, the selections will be grouped around themes of nature and its beauty, patriotism, colonial history, myths and legends, romantic love, and the era of independence and protest.

Finally, this editor wants to emphasize that the selections will be from various literary genres and that some selections will be excerpts from longer genres such as novels and/or short stories. Also, whenever selections are derived from the Garifuna language, the relevant English translation will be provided.

CHAPTER 1

Nature and its Beauty

Dawn is a Fisherman

By Raymond Barrow

Dawn is a fisherman, his harpoon of light
Poised for a throw — so swiftly morning comes:
The darkness squats upon the sleeping land
Like a flung cast-net, and the black shapes of boats
Lie hunched like nestling turtles
On the flat calm of the sea.

Among the trees the houses peep at the stars
Blinking farewell, and half-awakened birds
Hurtle across the vista, some in the distance
Giving their voice self-criticized auditions.

Warning comes from the cocks, their necks distended
Like city trumpeters: and suddenly
Between the straggling fences of gray cloud
The sun, a barefoot boy, strides briskly up
The curved beach of the sky, flinging his greetings
Warmly in all directions, laughingly saying
Up, up, the day is here! Another day is here!

From *Of Words: An Anthology of Belizean Poetry,* Belize, Cubola Productions, 1997, p.89

Tarde de Sol

Por Mary Gómez Parham

Serpiente sangrienta:
te deslizas sigilosa
por el subconsciente.

Brilla un sol nacido sin pecado original.
Sobre el verde limpio del césped
hay patos amarillos y niños de pelo dorado.
Sentimos el calor suave
de las plumas de los patos;
sentimos la piel lisa
de las caras de los niños.

Pero de pronto sentimos el frío hierro negro
de tu cuerpo bien engrasado
como herramienta del demonio.
Te acercas despacio y
ahora brotan manchas sucias
en el amarillo claro de los patos
y en el pelo dorado de los niños
salen canas plateadas.
Nos asombra ver que
la piel rosada de sus caritas redondas
se tuerce en mil arrugas:
surcos hondos llenos de pecados, secretos, lágrimas.

Ahora se alejan los niños de los patos manchados.
        Se extingue el sol
El verde húmedo del césped yace sombras.

Y allá donde el prado llega a la selva,
has sacado jubilosa tu larga lengua
        roja y salivosa

From *Of Words: An Anthology of Belizean Poetry*, Belize, Cubola Productions, 1997, p.92

Night - Mullins River

By Sir Colville N. Young

The water by the pier glows green:
Sea-dwellers' weird phosphoric light;
Five boats are waited for tonight;
Over the sea the wind whips, fresh and clean.

Snatches of conversation blown
Upon the breeze: "The Cosmo burst
A jib again, or would reach first,
But had to stay behind and get it sewn".

"Tomorrow Goddy Myvette giving
Big dance, music by boom-an-shine —
Plenty of boil-up, rum, and wine;
Couple excursions from Belize arriving".

"The young get drunk and carry on rude,
And can't dance waltz with a gentle touch."
"You older folks drink just as much,
And don't know how to dance the reggae good."

The boat-lights twinkle from afar —
The waiting hour is up at last;
Soon mainsails flap, and against the mast
sounds the hoarse creak and groan of lowering spar.

Conch-shells are blown with echoing shout;
Passengers, waiters, home-ward walk
To have their belly-ful of talk,
Then one by one the village lights go out.

From *Of Words: An Anthology of Belizean Poetry*, Belize, Cubola Productions, 1997, p.104

Ode To Ambergris Caye

By Nicholas A. Pollard Sr.

Beautiful Coral Crown
Maiden Isle of jewels rare
Befitting a free Belize!
White silvery beaches,
Green swaying coconut trees,
Aquamarine crystalline seas
Adorn your sandy beaches.

Pearl of the Caribbean,
With other gems of purest carat —
Which other earthly isle
Can I compare with you?

Conceived in the accumulation
Of coral bones and stones
Deceased in Poseidon's kingdom,
Silent went your slow gestation
Through millions and millions of eons!

Nestled in the warmth
Of tropic earth's moist womb,
Nurtured in her loins
You were slowly formed,
Until the baby isle was born,
O child from coral sprung!

The sea-birds brought you seeds
Of mangrove, grass and coco-plum;
The sun, the winds and rains,
They nurtured and they suckled you
Through babyhood and childhood,
To splendid, full-fledged islandhood —
The baby isle was babe no more!

You proudly wore your greenery,
The lobster and the oyster,
The snapper and the porpoise,
The angel fish and flying fish
All danced with joy about you
In primeval happy ribaldry!

Then came prehistoric Man
And vanished in the Flood.
The Maya and the Mosquito Indian
All sought your loving hand,
But all passed on.

Columbus sailed too far away,
His Spaniards knew you not;
Within your bosom pirates lay
Their treasure and their blood
They too passed on!

Baymen sons in forest hid
Ignored your regal beauty.
Then, lo! from far and wide
New Belizeans came
In quest of peace and love
And true prosperity!

The birds are singing in the trees,
Bells ring in the belfry,
The lobster and the oyster,
The snapper and the porpoise,
The grouper and the kingfish
Now dance with joy about you
In boundless happy rivalry!

O beautiful Coral Crown,
Maiden isle of jewels rare
Befitting our free Belize!

From *Belizean Poets Part 3*, Belize, Government Printers, (circa 1972)

Sub Umbra

By Leo Bradley

Shades and shadows manifold
Grace our tropic land;
silhouettes of sea-gull wings,
And palm shades on the sand;
Of countless coral windy cayes,
And dipping sail-boats grand.

House forms lie across the lanes
To ease the noon-day heat,
And bougainvilias lend their shade
While church spires lithely meet
The shadows of the shuffling soul
And the repentant feet.

And in the leafy forest home
Where bamboos bend beside
The silent streams, and timbers throw
Their massive forms and ride
Above the pine trees — there too
so many shades abide.

Yes, mid-day sunblaze, full-moon glow,
Send myriad shades to earth;
And we in humble confidence,
Through days of grief and mirth
Feel God's protective hands o'er shadow
Our blessed land of birth.

From *Belizean Flavour*, Belize, Spear Press, 1991

Wéyasu

By Marcella Lewis

Luagu aban weyu nadüga wéyasu
    Péinigien lun Córozali
Nágueir nagu
    Luagu bian louba üma
Anunhan sun túyeri ídibu
    Aruruha lóubawagu úma
        Bürü barihi
            Kamá le bunawaguárügütu.
Sun ídibu to
    Luntu taseriwiduníwa.
Banügei béyabugien anunhaya
    Tüyerigu ídibu
        Laru laru beya
Sun idibu to
    Lúntugien taseriwiduníwa
Káteisa gabafubei wéiribei ubafu
    Ábunagubaru ídibu to ítara ibe?
Marihíniwa lubéi luagu rügü
    Hamuga aban weyu ábunagua
Káteifunasa ábunaguti le Marihíbel?
Subuditisa hun nuéi?
Káteisa gabafuti le?
Niduheñu!
    Másura wamá saminara.
Máma dügü funasa
Wabureme Súntigabafu?
Samina humeisa numa.

Journey [English Translation]

One day I made a journey
    From Punta Gorda to Corozal.
I looked around
    From one side of the road to the other
All kinds of trees
    Right by the side of the road
        As far as you can see
            As if they were planted
All these trees
    Are good for us to use.
And turn towards the sea
    All kinds of trees
        Along the beach
All these trees
    Are good for us to use.
Who has the power
    To plant so many trees?
There is not a day
    When planting was seen
Who plants that is not seen?
Do you know so you may tell me?
Who is this powerful?
My people
    Let us not wonder
Was it not
    Our Master, the Almighty?
Think with me.

From *Walagante Marcella*, pp.24-25. Belize National Garifuna Council, 1994

Xunantunich

Por Yolanda Fuentes

Mute, lovely Maiden of the Rock
Whose mystery past we never mock
With cloud swept summit oh so high
And friendly travelers passing by
Midst shelters for fierce wind or rain
Fruits rim your boarders — citrus cane;
Flowers, and shrubs in uphill beat
Soft pedaling the tramp of weary feet.

Evening – and birds go screeching by
Home to secret places, way up high
Village children, singing in high pitch
To mother, home — and you XUNANTUNICH.

From *Belizean Poets, Part 3,* Belize, Government Printers, (circa), 1972, p. 30

The Precious Scene

By Sur Jim Arnold – B.A. (Bachelor of Antics)

A different sight

$\qquad\qquad\qquad\qquad$A better view
$\qquad\qquad\qquad\qquad$Is the Stann Creek valley
$\qquad\qquad\qquad\qquad$with morning dew.
$\qquad\qquad$With the sparkling, glistening, rising sunlight
$\qquad\qquad\qquad$Blessing down with God's delight.

Nature is here
No one feels lonesome
For there is the smell
Of the Citrus Blossom
Nothing can be compared
To its fragrance so dear
As it penetrates
The nasal pair.

$\qquad\qquad\qquad\qquad\qquad\qquad$As$\qquad$hundreds$\quad$of
parrots

$\qquad\qquad\qquad\qquad\qquad\qquad$Descending$\quad$for$\quad$the
feed

$\qquad\qquad\qquad\qquad\qquad$So$\quad$is$\quad$the$\quad$factories$\quad$blue
smoke

$\qquad\qquad\qquad\qquad\qquad$Ascending$\quad$twirling$\quad$with
speed

$\qquad\qquad\qquad$Light green hills
$\qquad\qquad$And deep blue mountains are there
$\qquad\qquad\qquad$Adding to the valley
$\qquad\qquad$Their beautiful surrounding share
$\qquad\qquad\qquad$Yes, there is green
$\qquad\qquad\qquad$The valley green
$\qquad\qquad$Surely this is the precious scene.

From *Kriol and English Poems Just for You, p6.* Peni Printers, Toledo, Belize, 1998

Herbs

By Sur Jim Arnold

You there!!!
   Talking about protecting our environment
   Protect this!!
Don't let them come in here,
cutting down our trees and our herbs
It might one day save your life.

      Thell them don't cut down Gombolimbo
      Mek them nuh mess wid mi Ceda Bark
      Show them which tree da Madre Kakow
      Give them tea from yuh Feva Grass

        Mek them nuh root up Jocoto
        Mek them nuh root up Kalalu
        Mek them nuh dig up yu Yama Bush
        Mek them respect wi Gengweheyo.

          Da weh yu deh Jan Charles
          Billy Web di look fu yu
          Da weh yu deh Jan Charles
          Billy Web di look fu yu.
                Tell them. Tell them

            Show them weh Sorosi can do
            Teach them weh Jack Ass Bitters fa
            Show them weh Palo Hombre deh
            Mek them meet Tala Wala

              Show them which da Kontreebo
              What is the use of Physic Nat
              Mek them know Apasote
              Introduce to them Stong Back

                Uña de Gato the Cat Claw
                Miracle cure for Asthma
                Stomach pain and Ulcer
                Leukemia and Cancer
                Miracle-cure-Miracle sure.

Ibid, p. 5

Egret

By Henry W. Anderson, MBBS JP

White flash has caught my eyes,
   A silver droplet in darkened skies;
   How godly to catch one fallen sunbeam
To send forth brilliance to the sky.
One cadenced sunbeam impales the darkened clouds
And sought and found you.
Be grateful bird
That the sun has made you
An envoy of its power.
Darkened clouds, how empty you are
When soft forward motion , oh egret,
Like lightening, bolts a thousand lights
Bursting forth from thy breast.
Oh egret! Bird of white,
Hold still lest the sunbeam lose you
And brilliance then forever gone.
But you go into darkened clouds;
Oh Egret — a silver droplet no more.

From *The Son of Kinich*, p. 39. Jaribu Books, Dangriga, Belize1995

Crab Seasin

By Evadne García

    Todeh, Belize City nuh stan like ih mih stan when wih dah mih pickney. Deh nevah gah no Bella Vista, all dehm pretty house deh, an dah king's Park mih nevah dih deh atahl. Dih city mih ehn right dah Fabah's Road junkshan. Dih Westan Highway mih nevah gah no light, an all who mi waahn waatah an mih nevah gah vat eenah deh yaad mih hafih guh dah stan-pipe.1
    Laahd,dih line suh lang, suhm bring dehn waatah bucket pahn kyaat, and eenah May, dih pipe hihn jus dih 'drip-drip.' While dehn gial dih 'shush,' we bwoy dih play cowboy, maable or caparuche 2.
    When dih Aagass rain finish, dih whole Belize City aandah waatah. Well, as wih mih dih deh pahn haliday, wih dicide fih guh ketch crab. Dih bes place fih mih ketch crab dehn dah mih up Fabah's Road. Billy, Jahn, and 'Spegle' she dehm mih gwine wid mih. Nuh badah fih try ketch crab if yuh nuh gah yuh crab ketching 'tools.'
    Yuh mus have hook, crocus beg an wahn kis-kis 3. Me? Ah gah home gahn beg Ma fih lem mih ih kis-kis. Sean seh hihn wah bring in Grampa crocus beg dehm. Wih mek wih hook frahn wah piece a close-line weh wih fine eenah Miss Mary yaad. Wih lef tung round ten a'clack. Now evri-bady know dat dih bes time fih ketch crab dah between ten dah mahning and two dah aftahnoon. Dis time dih waatah eenah dih hole dih bile; dehn kyaahn stay eenah deh, dehn hafl cuhm out pahn dih road! Wih waahk slow up Fabah's Road, evri way wih look wih sih crab-hole and crab . . ..
    Wehn wih pass Misah Coco Tee house, wih staat to ketch crab. Spegle dah dih fus wahn fih ketch wahn lee, chinchi crab. Dehn, evri-bady gahn crazy-crab fih days! Sudden wih heah Sean shout, "Bwoy, unuh cuhm yah, a sih wahn big bo. Dis wahn fih mih todeh; todeh, dis big clah gwine eenah soup."
    Billy seh, "Hook ah bwoy, Sean hook ahm."
    Sean call back, "Sumbady, bring dih kis-kis mek wih grab ah pahn ih back."
    Me?, I open ih crocus beg. Dis time, Sean pin dih crab an ih mi wah put ah eenah ih crocus beg wehn wih heah Jahn staat to laaf like ih simple.
    "Ha, ha, ha, Sean bwoy, dah weh duh yuh? Yuh hafi let dah wahn guh."
    "Yuh crazy or wat bwoy?...Dis dah dih biggis crab weh wih ketch todeh!", Sean seh.
    Now Jahn kyaahn hole up, "Sean, yuh nuh sih dah Wash Palm 4 yuh gah deh? Wih kyaahn ker dat home."
    Now evri-bady look pahn dah big brute good, dehn Billy ans Spegle really staat tooh laff fih troo. Yuh sih, Wash Palm crab gah ih egg pahn ih belly an dehn nuh tase nice. Sean mih really waahn dah crab, but it letih guh. Bout wahn-turty suh dih aftahnoon, wih mih gah at least ten crab each, suh wih decide fih guh home.
    Dis time, wih waakh dung dih Westan Highway frahm the junksham. Wehn wih reach dehm Indian pipple house, Jahn hihn decide fih guh get blackberries.

All a wih gahn up eenah dih tree an put Spegle fih watch fih Miss Rancharan.

Chuh, wehn wih staat tuh pick an eat ripe blackberry, nobady memebah she. Dis nex ting wih no, she stan up right andah dih berry tree...wid ih mule-whip eenah ih han!

Limb, branch an man scattah, dung dih road; only Jahn mih lef up eenah dih tree. Dih las ting wih yerri, dah ole Miss Rancharan dih she, "A ketch wahn ah unuh now, unuh lee brute. Yuh hafi cuhm dung an ah wah wait right yah fih yuh." Nobady look back, nobady stap-suhtay wih reach Laahd's Ridge's Cimitry. Nobady mih wah be dih fus or las fih guh eenah an lef deh!

Ten minits aftah wih reach Grampa house, wih sih Jahn dih cuhm. Ih seh. "Dih nex time unuh ruhn lef mih, a gwine tell Miss Rancharan dat dah yuh Billy, Sean and Clive, unuh mih foce mih fih climb ih berries tree."

Mah sen wih gahn bie tree pung a coco, wahn cucnat an foah green plaantin. Dah nite, wih eat lattah crab soup, wid plenty a Matilda foot 5.

Glassary

1. stan-pipe   Waatah facit fih dih hole dih village
2. caparuche   Pickney playing, wahn tap weh mek outah wahn piece ah
                 wood, ih shape like wahn cone an ih gah wahn nail inside. Fih
                 spin ah, ih gah wahn lang string weh fix pahn wahn battle
                 stappah.
3. kis-kis   "U" shape holdah weh mek outtah 'Puck-O-Nuh-Bwoy" treeh.
                 Ih use fih hat coal pahn dih fiah-haath.
4. Wash Palm   Laydih crab wid ih egg outside, pahn ih belly.
5. Matilda foot Dumplin frahm gratah green plantin, saal an ile.

From *Snapshots of Belize: an anthology of short fiction*. Ed. By Michael D. Phillips, Pp. 69-71. Cubola Productions, 1995. Belize, Central America

CHAPTER 2

Patriotism

Drums of my Fathers

By E. Roy Cayetano

To Ami, Vira and Isani: Eternally United by Blood and the Drums

Drums of my Fathers
Rumbling in my Bones—

            Organ Music

Drums of my Fathers
Beating in my mind—

            Jukebox blaring

Drums of my Fathers
Capturing my soul—

            Sing a hymn to Mary

Words of my Fathers
Tumbling from my mouth—

            Speak the Queen's English

Drums of my Fathers
    of my grandfather's
        of my ancestors
Drumming in my psyche
Drums of my Fathers
Drum! Beat!
      Beat on! Drum on!
            And on!

My Garifuna frame and
My Carib—
    bean bones tingle

Keeping time with the
Reverberating sounds
     of the hollowed trunk
     of the hollowed trunk
Whose roots reach deep in—
       to the hills
          and the vales
             and the streams
                and the soul
Of Africa   Reach in—
       to the banks
          and the waters
             and the heart
                and the mind

Of the Amazon
Of the Orinoco

My hybrid body shakes and
        sways and
        rocks and
        communicates

With the blur
     of wrinkled hands
     of hardened hands
With wrists still sore and scarred
      after manacles
        and cuffs
           and chains
     gunpowder and bullets
    and cross—
     shaped swords
That traversed the Atlantic
Calling at West African stations
And palm-island studs
     of the golden Antilles.

And like the antelope skin
That captured the clatter and the thunder
      of the hoofbeat
      of the herd
      in the African plains
And the rumble and the thunder
      of the jungles

and the falls
of the Amazon

I, stretched and taut,
Have taken the beating
        and the pounding:

But my spirit
            and my voice
Will not be quieted
Will not be muffled; for
I AM the hollowed
        hallowed
        haloed trunk
        and the hills and the vales
        and the streams and the soul
        OF AFRICA
            and the banks and the waters
            and the heart and the mind
OF THE AMAZON AND THE ORINOCO
            and the wrinkled calloused hands
            dragged across the Atlantic
            and dumped on the golden
            studs and shores
OF THE CARIB—
        BEING WATERS.

Yet, you must know,
I was here before all that,
I was here before—
        before
        the paler faces came;

And organ music
Jukebox blaring
Hymns sung to mary
and the quean's English
        shall not quiet the
Drums of my Fathers
Rumbling in my bones,
Drums of my Fathers
Capturing my mind,
Drums of my Fathers
Recapturing my soul, or the
Words of my Fathers
Tumbling from my mouth.

Drums of my fathers
        of my Grandfathers
        of my Ancestors
Drumming in my psyche
Soul of my Fathers
Drum! Beat!
        Beat on! Drum On!
                AND ON!

From *Of Words: An Anthology of Belizean Poetry*, pp. 32-35. Cubola Productions. 1997. Belize, Central America.

Belizeans: Unite to build our nation

By George C. Price

This tribute, to our Belizean patriots, is dedicated to our ancestors—those Belizeans, who in their day founded the new nation of Belize which in our day we build. Through us they live; and alive, they speak.

Builders, why do you stand looking out to sea?
We have worked all night and worked all day
building this new nation.
While we build, the rivers flood the roads,
the forests choke the tamed earth,
the underground waters flee the thirsty fields.
We have worked all day and worked all night.

The builders await the sunrise,
They seek new strength.
Building is a task for giants—
Little people tried and turned away.
The giant builders must save the land
and stay the creeping forests
and halt the fleeing waters.

The sun rises from the life-giving sea.
Its glory fills the beauty and the bounty
of our Belizean land.
There, the swampland;
There the rising, fertile plain;
Shining lake and glowing mountain,
Failure past, present growth and future greatness.

Belizean builders: see the living beauty
the teeming bounty, the soul-moving glory!
Look east whence rain clouds move inland
to quench the thirsty fields.
The sun's warmth and quickening rays
staunch the floor and enrich the fields.
Look west, Belizean builders. See the shining mountains
and the jeweled city of Mopan radiating
life and love and hope and joy!

From *Of Words: An Anthology of Belizean Poetry*, pp. 39-40. Cubola Productions. 1997. Belize, Central America

Hísienti Nageira Nun

By Marcella Lewis

Hísienti nageira nun
Ma nísebe sawanarugu
Fufu garabali
Wáwalu libian Súntigabáfu

Hísientima bei nun
Dan wásügürü tuaga lugunena müa
Ma lubuidu larumugu lídibu gudi
Sian warihini wübü
Darugua lau gúmulali

Aba nareiru lun néñeguhani
Nachülürü luagu wübü ni murusu watu ñei
Kása uéigien lagumulahábei, niduheñu,
Ligia úati watu luagu?
Aba nagiribudu, neredera lau saminaü

I love My Home [English Translation]

I love my home
How I love the savanna
I enjoy the sea breeze
With the sounds of the creatures of the Almighty

What I love the most
While we are passing in a bus
Is how beautiful the leaping of the pine trees
We cannot see the mountains
They are covered in smoke

I get out to put out the fire
When I get to the mountain there is no fire
Why is there smoke, my people
And there is no fire?
I turn back in wonder.

From *Walagante Marcella, Marcella Our Legacy*, p. 29. National Garifuna Council, 1994. Caye Caulker, Belize.

Lef mi ya

By Patricia Sánchez

Yuh tell me fuh go waak wit yuh da States
It nice an so. Da no wan place weh I hate.
But deh, I feel too pen up. I no feel free.
I kiant tek mi strol by di beach, and watch mi Caribbean sea.

Yuh neva want mek I com, but Belize da mi home.
Weh I cud eat nice janny cake, creole bread and bun.
 Pon twelve o' clock mi rice 'n beans; boil plantin or hudut
Or maybe, curry, corn tortillas, beans, sere or matilda fut.

Yuh tink unu hav meat, try fuh we markeet.
It have pigtail, pikary, deer-meat and steak.
Pon top, conch, lobster, chickin, pork, gibnut an gwana.
All kinda fish, like snappa, jack, shark, barro an crana.

Yuh taak bout different race, gial Belize da di place.
From Nart to Sout, East to west, yuh see all kinda face.
We have Creole, Garifuna, Mestizo, Ketchi, Maya, Indian and Mennonites.
Even East Indians, Turks an Chiney di unite.

I like me lee contry bad
Although wen tings get haad, I feel real sad.
But lef mi ya da Belize, No cal me fu go no way.
Because even if I go, I no gwine deh long fu stay!

From *Belizean Poets, Part 3*, p. 37. Government Printers, Belize . (Circa, 1972)

Excerpt from __Got seif de Cuin__!

Por David Nicolás Ruiz Puga

... Los invasores nunca llegaron; y cuando don Enrique salió con el cuento de que habían sido vendidos a los Ingleses, y que él se había vuelto el Representante de La Corona Británica en el pueblo, le hicieron poco caso. El viejo no logró consolidar su puesto de máxima autoridad hasta que don Justo falleció, en la víspera de la Solemnidad del Apóstol Santiago, en que se bailaban los Moros y Cristianos en la plaza frente a la iglesia.

Don Justo había sido el único alcalde desde muchos, muchos años atrás. Todos sabían que él era el único de los sobrevivientes de la mística ciudad del Tipú, perdida en el tiempo, donde crecían mazorcas con granos de oro y donde Chaac bajaba a regar las siembras con gotas cristalinas de jade imperial.

Al darse cuenta del vacío que la ausencia del líder dejaba, el pueblo buscó amparo con don Enrique. Este no vaciló en tomar acción. Al cabo de veinticuatro horas ya tenía el cuerpo de don Justo en el hoyo, para que todo el mundo le diera el último homenaje con su terrón de tierra negra.

Al terminar el entierro, el viejo con cuerpo de saramuyo se agachó cuidadosamente y tomó con mucha dignidad una masa pequeña de tierra, y la tiró sobre el montículo. Luego, tomó la cruz de palo donde se leía: DON JUSTO – EL ULTIMO DE LOS CHAN y la colocó al pie de la tumba. Entonces, levantando su bastón de oro con las dos manos y con la mirada penetrante hacia el horizonte exclamó con vigor y autoridad, la frase que el hombre blanco, con el ojo de vidrio, le había hecho repetir cien veces: "Got seif de Cuin!"

La gente consternada se quedó viendo los unos a los otros, y los niños se asomaban temerosamente detrás de las enaguas de las madres. Algunos se reían entre dientes y otros llegaban a la conclusión de que al viejo enjuto se le habían "subido los humos" a la cabeza.

El nuevo alcalde decretó diez días de duelo con ayunos y oraciones por la muerte del último sobreviviente del Tipú. Se instaló en el Cabildo y colgó en la pared, detrás de la mesa de autoridad, el retrato de la señora con madrileña, que había encontrado en su mesa, dos días después del incidente con el hombre blanco de ojos color de cielo.

Al poco tiempo nombró a seis comisionados, entre ellos a su primo hermano, aquél que vivía en Plancha de Piedra, en el área de Fayabón, al otro lado del río, para que le ayudaran a mantener el orden y la paz en territorio de Su Majestad.

Un día en que don Enrique salía del cabildo para convocar la fajina tradicional del día de Finados, le llegó la noticia de que el hombre blanco estaba en la región, y que visitaría el poblado. El alcalde no perdió ni un segundo en mover al pueblo entero para recibir con honores al señor que les mandaba azúcar fina, galletas inglesas, casimir para los flux, y crinolinas para los vestidos. Convocó a la gente en la plaza e hizo saber que la fajina del día de Finados se reservaría para limpiar la calle principal. Luego, dio a conocer el programa de recepción que había preparado junto con los comisionados. El viejo en pantalón y camisa de manta levantó su bastón para conseguir la atención del público, y echando un escapulario al suelo dijo:

"El día 30 se convocará al pueblo entero al repique de campanas pa' que se reunan en la entra'a, allá por la matanza pa' encontráa al hombre blanco con el ojo de vidrio y a su comitiva. . . le pido a to'os los que viven de la matanza a la plaza, que adornen sus casas con arcos y corozo . . . encabezarán el encuentro don Dolores y don Prisciliano segui'os por niños y niñas de escuela, portando banderines y flores, dirigi'os por las Hermanas del Convento, segui'os por la marimba de don Felipe . . . y de allí, las señoras y señores dirigi'os por don Rito y don Adolfo, segui'os por otra marimba . . .. "

La gente murmuraba mientras don Enrique hablaba ceremoniosamente, gesticulando con su bastón en mano.

"¡Ah! Casi se me olvida . . . " siguió el viejo estirando el pescuezo, "les comunico que don Felipe le ha cambiado el nombre a su marimba . . . ahora se llama La Británica y será la marimba que tocará la pieza de bienvenida Ave Lira . . . ¡así pues, que el que se oiga llamándole Ecos Españoles a la marimba de don Felipe, tendrá que afrentarse a las consecuencias!"

La gente quedó perpleja. Don Enrique paseó la mirada sobre el pueblo entero y encogiéndose de hombros vociferó: "Ni mo'os . . . la ley lo exije . . . Got seif de Cuin!"

Dicho esto, el viejo se dio la vuelta y se metió al Cabildo. Entre murmullos de que Dios le había dado alas a ciertos alacranes, la gente se dispersó para ver como le hacían para que sus casuchas de lodo y coloshché cambiaran de apariencia para el hombre del ojo de vidrio.

From *Got seif de Cuin*, pp. 12-14. Editorial Nueva Narrativa. Guatemala, 1995

Esta es mi Tierra

Por Edison Coleman

Por el sur y por el norte
El poniente y occidente,
Lucharemos por hacerte
Belice, independiente.

O Belice patria mía,
Trabajemos noche y día,
Y muy pronto, si Dios lo quiere
Diremos, "Esta es mi tierra."

Ya tus símbolos tenemos,
No hay por qué nos marchemos,
Hombro a hombro, sí marchemos,
¡Libertad así logremos!

Por tus ríos y tus valles,
Por tus montes y tus calles,
¡Belice! Unidos donde quiera
Digamos, "Esta es mi tierra!"

From *Of Words: An Anthology of Belizean Poetry*, p. 49. Cubola productions,
Belize, Central America, 1997.

Dis Da Me

By Philip Lewis

Who seh Belize people culture weak?
Now don't behave like Brownman mule
"Fish come form river bottom, tell you
            alligator got belly ache"
Doh ee sound like fool, believe am

Miss Gladys, Sefe and Tata du Hende
Mek you laugh when you hear who is the real bemeb
Miss Floss and Chi Chin with a tune and a stick
Educate you with sense more than cobo and Plick

Da true "Every John Crow think ee pickney white"
Maybe dat's mek Spaniards start to fight
With a claim which up to today day
Tonio, Price nor Goldson brush away

When yu want to know a person pedigree
Question a neighbour who lives close by he
Run off bout logwood, Battle a St. George's Caye
and a solid junk a slave a ree

Grampa know pit pan, Cayo boat, barbeque
Granny pataki, chamberpot and John cu nu
Seven an foh, "gang-bruck" during christmas time
Mean turkey, ham and bram and Boom 'N Chime

Powder bun, fry-fish and Johnny cake
Outside fire-hearth, fire-coal ready to bake
Plantain, creole bread or bun a full pot
of rice and beans and who Papa Craig got

Sorosi, chickle tree, maca pal out west
Coolie Indian curry, Fu fu, Garifuna feast
Why you no contact old people if you need a
good teacher
to clear all your doubts about a Belizean culture.

From *Of Words: An Anthology of Belizean Poetry*, pp. 47-48. Cubola
Productions, Belize, Central America, 1997

Remembering

Anonymous

Close your eyes and go back
Before the Internet and the Mac
Before semi-automatics and crack,
Before Hattieville and Ramada
And all the problems with Guatemala,
Before SEGA or Super Nintendo
When life was simple and air conditioning was your open window.
Go way, way back.

O, I'm talking about playing hide and seek at dusk,
Sitting on the veranda, eating hot Creole bread and butter.
Seferino, Eustace Usher and Everall Waight on Radio Belize.
Red light, Green light (those are games we had no traffic lights in Belize).
Powder milk (AKA Klim) and a potted meat sandwich for lunch was dandy.
Kottobrute, tableta, stretch-mi-guts, wangla and goatshit for candy
Boil corn and ducuno from Fullmoon Bevas on Hydes Lane.
Macobi (pepitos) seeds from Bredda Roy or Don Marín at Holy Redeemer.
Playing caparuche or gamma in the neighbour's yard,
Hopscotch, marbles, ludo, snake and ladder, Jacks, cricket,
Mother May I, Say, Say, Say and Ring around the Roses.
Hula Hoops and racing bicycle rims.
Bradley's lemonade (all flavors were lemonade)
And 2 panades for 5 cents
Dit's meat pies (1 for 5) and Happy Hour's cow foot soup (only 35).
Black shoe polish on mustaches to get into Eden, Majestic or Palace,
Crossing kinnel iron, a nude dip at barracks.
The smell of the sun and lickin salty lips.

Wait....
10:30 Sunday morning matinee, Superman, The Three Stooges and Bugs.
Back further, listening to reverend Matthew and Chichi on the radio.
Catching needle cases (never knew their real names) off the clothes line,
Making your own kites with kite paper from Angelus Press and flour paste.
Making sure roaches wouldn't eat your kite by putting kerosene on the paste.
Playing sling shot or using rubber bands with orange peeling to sting maclala.
Remember when walking from New Road to New Market seemed far away?
And going downtown on Albert Street seemed like going somewhere?
Ghost stories at bedtime, climbing trees, gathering black berries and mangoes.

An ice cream cone from one-eye Mallick on a hot summer day,
Tuti-Fruti, Sour Sap or maybe Sugar Corn.

You found this other eye, you say?
A burger and coke from Shammah's drug store on Queen Street,
A million mosquito bites , flit, fish (for mosquitoes) and sleeping under nets.
Kerosene lamps, gas lamps and candles.
Etnas (one-holed kerosene stoves), chamber pots and the good old white bucket.
Cops and Robbers, Cowboys and Indians, playing house (oooh, I liked that).
Steve Reeves and Gordon Scott, when all leading actors were "the bwai,"
Sitting on the fence whistling at girls passing by.
Sliding down the rail of the steps, catching a splinter on your ass.
Jumping on the bed (if you had one) and pillow fights.
Running from Catate and Dilo till you were out of breath,
And laughing so hard that your stomach hurt.
Being tired just from playing. Remember that?

I'm not finished just yet.
Eating Klim with sugar, kawsham too.
Remember when...
The sneakers at Bata for boys and girls were called puss?
And you were ashamed to wear them at school cause they only cost a dollar?
When it took five minutes for the transistor radio to warm up?
And you listened to championship fights and that was fun?
When nearly everyone's mom was at home when the kids got there?
When every kid owned some type of dog?
And how you cried when they poisoned yours?
When five cents was a decent allowance, and ten cents a miracle?
When Saldivar bread went up two cents and everyone talked about it for weeks?
When you lined up outside Jail at 5:00 AM for hot jail bread?
When you'd reach into a stinking, muddy drain for a penny?
When girls neither dated nor kissed until late high school?
And juking behind convent or up by Haulover was cool?
When girls wore quindolyn to church every Sunday?
And your clothes were always clean and pressed,
Even though you didn't have many?
And we'd all have to be at the 8:30 AM mass on Sunday or else?
When you got brawta from the grocery store regardless of how much you
bought?
And 12 cents American cheese and a pack bread fed a family of 8?

When laundry detergent had free glasses, dishes or towels hidden inside a box?
When any parent could whap any kid and nobody, not even the kid gave any
thought?
When being sent to the principal's office was nothing compared to the fate that
awaited you at home?
When you wore two or more pairs of short pants under your long pants to

Ease the sting from that sash corn or tambram whip from one of your male teachers?

When we were in fear of our lives but it wasn't because of drive-by-shootings, drugs, gangs etc.?

When our parents and grandparents were a much bigger threat?

When you didn't talk back to your parents, at least not to their face?

Didn't that feel good? Just to go back and say, yeah, I remember that!

There's nothing like the good old days!

They were good then,

And they are good now when we think about them.

The New Spirit

By Glenn Godfrey

The sun has arisen across the Mayan hills,
And in the morning light a Maya tills,
Upturning with each blow rich virgin soil,
Not a minute spent in else but toil.

His tools are ancient as the crops he sows,
And ancient are the hands which guide the hoe,
but what new light in those old eyes now gleams,
A new rising, some new hope it seems.

No longer does he work without an aim,
And days which once to him were all the same,
And milestones to a goal which had been vain,
for Mopan is arising now again.

A thousand white men came from off the sea
Ten thousand Negroes wanting to be free,
And in the North bloodthirsty Indians chased,
Mestizoes down to Belize all in haste.

The Mayas who with patience work the land,
Tall Caribs with a harpoon held in hand,
Lived side by side and yet so far apart,
With not a common dream to bind the heart.

But now there is a spirit in the land,
And all the races join in hand in hand,
Their task-to build a nation that is free,
A young new nation born in liberty.

So now the Maya tills with newborn zeal
And white-men, black-men shouldering the wheel
From bricks of faith they build a nation grand
And mortar it with sweat from work worn hands.

From *Of Words: An Anthology of Belizean Poetry*, pp. 41 & 42. Cubola Productions, Belize, Central America, 1997.

Garinagu Sarawama: Chülüha dan

By Marcella Lewis

Garinagu sarawama
Chülüha dan
Ñübiwama lidoun aban
Hurawamei fanidira
Iñurawaméi wamalali
Keimoun wabaronguoun

Garinagu mágurawaméi wanasiun
Adimurehawaméi wereru
Pántawama lau wereru niduheñu
Gamalaliwama aganbúa wamamuga
Daralamuga bena wabá
     lun webelurun luei huya
Buchá wawagu áhuyua
Wasanigu Garinagu, eyeriun, hianruin,
Dúgúwama wideha luagu lawanseru
     wageira
Haranseha wayunagu wabá.
Lun súdara badíüla háratiun,
Luyawa, lemenigirame wageira
     le Balisi,
Wabien, libime wabien.

Garinagu Arise: The Time has Come.

[English Translation]

By Marcella Lewis

Garinagu arise
The time has come
Be as one
Wave our flag
Raise our voice
Let us go forward!

Garinagu, let us not abandon our roots
Let us speak our language
Let us be proud of our language, kinfolks
Let us have a voice so we may be heard
So the door may be open for us to come in
    from the rain
We are tired of being in the rain.
Our Garifuna children, boys and girls,
Let us stand and help in the advancement
    of our homeland
Established for us by our ancestors
You must be brave soldiers,
Guardians, and support our homeland,
    Belize,
Our home, sweet home.

From *Walagante Marcella, Marcella Our Legacy*, pp. 4 & 5. National Garifuna Council, 1994, Caye Caulker, Belize.

Excerpt from **Guerras y Rumores de Guerra**

Por David N. Ruiz Puga

Tres días después de la partida de don Emilio Awde, apareció una nota en la puerta de la casa de don Chencho. Llevaba un mensaje escrito con puño y letra del viejo. Hablaba de sus contactos y de la ocupación *Kaibil*. Según la misiva, la ocupación duraría solamente una semana, pues las fuerzas aliadas desalojarían al invasor en un abrir y cerrar de ojos; y, mientras tanto, aquellos renuentes a no irse del pueblo, deberían meterse debajo de la cama cuando comenzara la guerra, ya que las bombas no pasarían por el colchón. Nadie supo en donde se escondió don Chencho.

El pueblo entero se convirtió en un cementerio. Las pocas almas permanecieron esperanzados a que don Chencho y la lógica tuvieran razón. Mi papá habló de algunas cuevas camino a *Camp Six* donde podíamos refugiarnos, por si comenzaban a caer las bombas, pero mi madre dijo que preferiría mil veces irse de cocinera de los invasores a terminar encerrada en una cueva. Sin embargo, la vida marchó como de costumbre. Mi abuelo continuó enseñando películas de guerra en su cine y el Coronel dando sus bailes en le Salón verde de Fallabón. Los gallos y las gallinas terminaron sus días en las ollas de escabeche y relleno negro, y la verdad, se gozó de una tranquilidad que jamás se había vivido en el pueblo.

A los dos meses, cuando la invasión resultó ser fabricación de un haragán quien solamente deseaba comerse los pollos, comenzaron a regresar las caravanas de gente moribunda, afligida con la malaria contraída en el norte. El alcalde regresó con los brazos cruzados sin tener donde caer muerto, pues había vendido todas sus pertenencias antes de irse. El Juez de Paz no volvió a verse; la caja de cartón donde llevaba los huesos de doña Eustaquia fue encontrada dos años después por el cura a la puerta de la iglesia y una misiva con las palabras: *la guerra no es para los que quieren descansar en paz.* A don Chencho lo hallaron tieso en su excusado muerto de asfixia. Los refugiados de Fallabón regresaron mucho tiempo después contando historias de Juanchón, el duende que veían volando en las cuevas cuando comían los hongos rosados del tamaño de un paraguas en las paredes musgas y húmedas, muy dentro de la tierra.

Los invasores nunca llegaron. Río Viejo consiguió su independencia de Gran Bretaña, y los tanques de guerra continuaron llegando al cementerio viejo del pueblo. Doce años después, cuando las tropas británicas sacudieron los pies de Río Viejo, el testimonio de un ex-oficial de Fallabón confirmó que los cuentos de don Chencho no eran puros cuentos. Era cierto; se había esperado la palabra de don General de la República para invadir Río Viejo aquel verano, cuando todos en el pueblo dormimos debajo de las camas.

Mi abuelo aún seguía llegando a la casa cada domingo a eso de las 7:00 de la noche a esperar la hora de la Misa. Cuando la televisión por cable invadió el pueblo, decidió cerrar el cine y frecuentar más la iglesia. Aún habla de las guerras y de los rumores de guerra, recordando la desesperación y el pánico de la gente.

—El col de este litigio se cocinó entre la Gran Bretaña y España, —volvió a decir aquella noche cuando se comentaba la noticia del día. El ejército de mil efectivos de Río Viejo había tomado las riendas de la defensa del país, y recibirá trece millones de dólares al año del presupuesto nacional para su mantenimiento—¡Somos ya un pueblo aparte, los ingleses ya se largaron a la mierda! ¡Nos llevamos con los de Fallabón! ¡Centroamérica se está desmilitarizando y se respira paz y seguridad por dondequiera! –Afianzó su sombrero de fieltro sobre la cabeza y se levantó. —¿Oyeron lo que pasó allá en San Joaquín?—murmuró sin darle la mirada a nadie;— ¡dicen que apareció el rostro de Jesús en la pared! ¡Ha de ser una señal! —Aplastó su cigarro en el cenicero y, sin despedirse, caminó erguido hacia afuera..

From *La Visita* by David N. Ruiz Puga. México: Ediciones Pleamar, 2000, pp. 104-106.

Our Flag

By Gilroy Usher

The blue, white and red flag flies high and free
We love to see it in cities, in villages and on every caye
It is our flag; so it is the Belizean flag, and we are proud of it
It symbolizes an independence that is to our benefit
Under it we support and build Belize with greater effort.

Our flag shows thanks to God for our waters and our fertile lands
It expresses thanks to God for our buildings, our products
And our highlands
Our flag says thanks to God for every Belizean and all our
Plants and animals
It utters thanks to God for protecting us from Guatemalan generals
For the only Belize our blue, white, and red flags says thanks
To the Lord our God

Our flag watches as we pay our taxes and do our work with vigour
Under it we build bridges, make larger milpas, and export sugar
Our flag displays our unity as together we build Belize with dignity
As we raise our flag together, all over Belize developments are conducted
together
Strict, we build better homes, hospitals, factories, army
Bases and schools in every district.

The colours of our flag mean that Belize is the home of
Belizeans, expectancy and democracy
The presence of our flag gives us courage for challenging steps forward
Better off under it, we see that colonialism kept Belize backward
With our flag and prayers we praise our late leaders and
Inaugurate each important thing
Our future generations will wave our flag as they
Continue to develop Belize and sing.

From *Belizean Poets Part 3*, Belize: Government Printers, circa 1972, p. 40

Independent Belize 1982

By Jacqueline Sutherland (née Fuller)

'Twas only a year ago today
Amid the sound of hip hip hip hooray
Shared was the joy of this beautiful nation
As it became independent with much jubilation.

Ministers, citizens, children and all
Had responded when they heard the call
And lo! After years of toil and dedication
Independence was reached—a time for celebration.

Peace, love and unity reigned
The long-sought for goal had been attained
Onward Belize—Forward Belizeans
Honour your national creations.

Show respect for your flag
On your national heritage place a tag
Be proud of your symbols and signs
You are living in independent times.

Whether middle-aged—young or old
See that your history is told
To countrymen or foreigner have it sold
Whatever the cost you must be bold.

No longer the need of parental support
With other countries good political rapport
Now the need for hard work and dedicated labour
Then soon all the struggles will be over.

Remember it is sweet to be independent
Of particular joy to be no longer dependent
So as we celebrate September twenty-first
Let courage, peace and unity be a mist.

And throughout our times of celebration
Let us show signs of re-dedication
Belize for Belizeans ever
On with the Independence celebrations-together forever.

From *Belizean Poets*, Part 3. Belize: Government Printers, circa 1972, p. 44

Super High

By Evan X Hyde

I'm the son of a buccaneer
and a black woman
I'm the son of a Spanish man
and a Carib woman
I'm the son of a Creole man
and an Indian woman
I'm the son of an English
    Soldier
and a mingo whore
I'm the son of love
I'm the son of sex
I'm the son of violence
Damn you, racial purist
I am Belize

I am the shining sun
I'm black, sucker
I'm gold and brown
and white and yellow
and bad
I'm the burning sun
fool
I'm cooking and
I'm smoking
I'm going to eat your head off
crush your ribs
kick out your seed
son of a bitch
you gon find out

From: *Of Words: An Anthology of Belizean Poetry,* Edited by Michael D. Phillips. Belize: Cubola Productions, 1997, p. 53

Our Country

By Alice Kirkwood

I love the high stars of the West,
I love the Northern Sugar Cane,
I love the harbours of the East,
I love the high hills of the South.

No matter if I never see,
The New Belize that lies ahead,
I know it is my Native land,
And I must love it evermore.

The men who labour by the sea,
The farmers who awake and work,
The Premier and his Ministers,
Are all Belizeans like me.

We lift our eyes and see the flag,
That flies above our Native land;
We love our country and our God,
Who makes it strong and rare and free.

This Land I Love

By Leo Bradley

'Midst the brilliant, flick'ring shadows
Of a tropic, moonlit night,
Have I gazed in dazzled wonder,
Where in scenery of delight—
Clouds of happy, waving palm trees
Court the azure skies above,
While the frothy , emerald wavelets
Dash upon this land I love.

Many summers have I wandered
Far across enchanted lands,
That are decked with pirate mysteries;
And upon whose grainy sands
Of a hundred sun-bathed islets,
Or in forest did I rove
Wrapt in glorious admiration
For this blessed land I love.

Streams and steamlets vie in beauty,
Rushing to the Carib Sea;
Cooling lands of tropic verdure
Where in peace a people free
Dwell in calm, serene and lasting
And admire the olive dove
And with shoulder bent to shoulder
Marches on this land I love.

Proud am I to bear the birth-mark
Of this sunny, sacred soil,
Which fore-fathers of the ages,
Bent and built in fervid toil;
And if e'er a patriot prosper,
'Neath our country's skies above—
I shall be the one to answer
For this blessed land I love!

Chapter 3

Colonial History

Excerpt from X Communication

Knocking our own Ting

By Evan X Hyde

My Ancestors and Your Ancestors

The masters of any society, legitimate or illegitimate, have the power to shape the historical accounts of events in order to suit their ends. Our slavemasters have been the English people—Caucasians. They write history books which lie to us in order to bluff, blind and deceive us. They have successfully created and maintained division amongst the black, brown, red and yellow people of our society in order to rule us. The so-called "Creole" and so-called "Spanish" tribes in our country have confronted each other with animosity for decades now. The slavemaster loved the bickering and distrust between two enslaved people. As long as we could not get together on the basis of having a common enemy—him—the situation was to his liking. No one can deny that the most effective historical source of division between the tribes in our society has been the so-called Battle of St. George's Cay. Utilizing brilliant historical propaganda, the English over a period of time passed the credit for the "defeat" of the Spanish from the white Baymen to the Negro slaves. The 10th became a Creole holiday subsidized and encouraged by the English. The myth was created that white master and black slave fought hand in hand against a dastardly aggressive tyrant—the Spaniard. For the black masses, the 10th is another excuse to get high. For the sycophantic Creole bourgeoisie class, the 10th represented a legitimization of their supremacy in the civil service administrative circles of government. The "negroes" were supposed to be the victors. For the English, the 10th has been an opportunity to divide the native society by allying themselves with the Creole bourgeoisie class against the "niggers" and the "Pania" and the "Kerobi." You can understand why the Creole bourgeoisie who are in opposition to the government were so aroused when there was an attempt to "discredit" the "battle of St. George's Caye." This was an attack on, as they saw it, the legal historical foundation of their right to be an exploiting class. For us the black people, the 10th as I have said, is an excuse to get high. It never mattered that much to us whether we defeated the Spanish or not because we certainly had not gained anything by it. We were living bad and the English people were living good. Our parents and grandparents joined the P.U.P.[1] because they were anti-English. They could not be fed any "master and slave, black man and white listed and counted as brave" jazz. They knew white people (English) did not dig black people. Of course they were betrayed because they did not know that white people (American) hated niggers even more and thus Price led us from English colonialism into American imperialism. But the betrayal is not the point now.

What matters is that because of the system as it has existed, no attempt has ever been made to interpret 1798, from the black man's standpoint.

Now we know that we hated the slavemaster's guts enough in 1773 to execute six of them in a rebellion. We know every slave who is a man and every slave who is a woman hates the master.

From *X Communication* by Evan X Hyde. Belize City: The Angelus Press, 1995. pp. 1-2

Excerpts from the Maya Atlas

How can we, Mayas, be considered immigrants? We are the original inhabitants of Toledo, [in the south] Belize who know no boundaries. The concept of putting down boundaries is European.

The Maya and the Ke'kchi Mayas have always lived in harmony until the coming of the Europeans. Our religious beliefs and traditions are the same. The concept of one ethnic group being superior to the other started when the Europeans began their Christianization crusade. The Ke'kchi resisted Christianization more than the Mopan. The Chrisatinized Mopan were made to feel superior to the "pagan" Ke'kchi. Thus began the rule of divide and conquer. [p.2]

The mayas of Toledo are the direct descendants of the ancient Mayas whose civilization reached its peak around A.D. 900. The continuous use of the Maya temples for religious purposes is testimony to their connection with the past. Present-day Mopan Maya descendants were found living in the vicinity of the Moho River by the Spanish missionaries, and present-day Mopan and Ke'kchi Mayas speak about the Christianization ordeal in Punta Gorda Town. Many of the Mayas who refused to be Christianized fled into the interior to take refuge in the Maya Mountain range. The Mopan call these people *Che'il* and the Ke'kchi call them *Chol*.

Both Ke'Kchi and Mopan continue to look up to these unconverted Mayas. They speak to their leaders through prayers and incense burning, exhorting their names—*Wal Itza*, *Wal Shucaneb*, *Wal Taca* and *Wal Cua*. These Mayan leaders are considered to be the caretakers of wild animals. They live in caves and were often contacted in the past to assist hunters and chicle workers. Present-day Mayas speak of their contact with them during the period of mahogany and chicle operators. Whem workers came down from the forest for Christmas or Easter vacation, the forest would become silent, and the few Mayas who stayed behind speak of seeing Mayan children cracking cohune nuts on food trails used by mahogany workers. A few chicle workers speak of being assisted by these wild Indians in bleeding of chicle trees in return for salt. Hunters have also met these *Che'il* and made secret agreements to exchange meat for salt.

From *Maya Atlas*, North Atlantic Books: Berkley, California, 1997, pp. 2 &3

Excerpt from La Visita

Por David Ruiz Puga

La escuela Católica Romana de San José contaba con varios alumnos de Fallabón, quienes cruzaban la frontera diariamente con el propósito de recibir una educación en inglés. Cada día, al tocar la campana del recreo, íbamos a comprar los dulces de melcocha y nos sentábamos bajo el árbol de *bucut* para hablar de los rumores de Guerra. Esto nos provocaba una especie de miedo y ansiedad que terminaba en discusiones y alegatas con los de Fallabón. Fabricábamos una Guerra sangrienta entre soldados blancos, cuyos antecesores se habían destacado durante la Segunda Guerra Mundial, y los *Kaibiles* de Fallabón que eran entrenados rigurosamente en las densas selvas por expertos israelitas para entrar en combate solamente en situaciones de emergencia. Zumbaban por los cielos aviones *Harriers* de la Fuerza Aérea de Su majestad, más rápido que el sonido; y avanzaban por la tierra tanques de acero aplastando las barreras de piedra del destacamento en la frontera. Le dábamos vida a las imàgenes de las muchas películas de guerra vistas en la pantalla grande del cine, en donde los blancos siempre vencían al enemigo. Los de Fallabón hablaban de los tanques anfibios y de su ejército de trescientos mil efectivos *Cuques* que manejaban los machetes como cucharear los frijoles. Hacían alarde de la fuerza *Kaibil;* sus soldados combatían en la selva por días sin alimento alguno. En plena masacre, nos poníamos a pensar en nuestra suerte. Mientras los del pueblo hablábamos de irons al norte hacia la frontera de Yucatán, los de Fallabón hacían mención de unas cuevas más allá de las montañas donde había suficiente agua y espacio. La discusión terminaba cuando sonaba la campana y todos acordábamos en irnos a las cuevas en caso de Guerra.

Esa era la preocupación de todos, la agresión bélica de los *Kaibiles* de Fallabón a través de la frontera occidental, a dos millas del pueblo.—¡Es su obligación comer carne de chucho, es parte de su entrenamiento pa'probar su resistencia!—decía la tía Emilia cuando nos visitaba de Fallabón y comenzaba a hablar del ejército *Kaibil* que había establecido su base militar al otro lado de la frontera con el nombre "El Infierno." Como decía la hermana de mi abuela, los militares solamente esperaban oír el grito de guerra de don General de la República. Cruzarían la frontera con machetes y ametralladoras para recuperar el territorio que, según el General, le pertenecía a Fallabón por el *Uti Possidetis*, el derecho de la excolonia española a los territorios dentro de las fronteras coloniales, dada su independencia política. –Dicen que acá, en Río Viejo, se detuvo el proceso de la evolución de las especies, y todos viven como puro frijol negro en olla, rascándose la barriga todo el santo día,—continuaba la tía Emilia refiriéndose a las conversaciones que oía al otro lado de la frontera;—¡Les digo, a esos militares debemos tenerles miedo, nos pueden caer encima

en cualquier momento! ¡están esperando la orden de allá arriba!—Mi madre la
miraba y sonreía.—¡Tonterías, tía!—decía sin dejar sus quehaceres;—¡si el
General apenas puede con su gente!—

From *La Visita* by David N. Ruiz Puga. México: Ediciones Pleamar, 2000, pp. 96-97

My People Came Here

By Roland A. Parks

My people came here
to this wilderness
of human-winter.
My people came here
far from the romantic
caresses of the sun's light
far from the passionate
calling of the sea.

My people came here
as strangers
seeking exile
from the inflaming embrace
of poverty
mocking their existence
in the dust of dying streets.

My people came here
now they are being
digested
into the stomach of
another madness.
The chains they still
drag here
on the cold floors
in-difference
to the march of time
to the red of blood
beneath the black of skin.

My people came here
where no blue reef
kiss the lips
of the horizon
only drying smokes
of broken dreams
vaporizing into
the geography of their illusive
obscurity.

My people came here
as one flower
from the tree of life,
now they are scattered
like distant echoes
from the sorrowful
voice of time.

My people came here
now of my homeland
naught now remain
save the call of poverty
louder than the discontent
voices of those
who betrayed a
revolution
far away and long ago.

From *Belizean Poets, Part 3*. Government Printers: Belize, Central America, 1972, pp. 13-14

Belice, mi Belice

Por Natividad Obando

A medio paso me detuve
Pa no estorbar el momento
En respiración profunda
Este concepto de arte recibí.

Lo vi. Lo vi. Sí.
Lo vi en mi más alto pensar
El medio de un silencio harmónico
Rodeado con aura de rayos de plata.
Belice mi Belice lo vi libre . . .

Cansado de este arduo viaje,
Regresé otra vez en sí.
Y fue difícil y en vano
Ignorar pa no aceptar.

"Todo es posible" susurré diciendo
Pa aquel que vive en mí
Que él consiga la plata
Y el oro que es un tesoro.

Pues lo que ven frente a ustedes
Es lo que mis manos rindieron
El oro se convirtió en madre cacao
Los rayos de plata salen de vuestros ojos
Las leyes que gobiernan vienen del más allá
Son perfectas, rectas y eternas
Y si el secreto de ello quieren saber
Luz, vida y amor tendrán que tener.

From *Belizean Poets, Part 3*. Government Printers: Belize, Central America, 1972 p. 39

Excerpt from Belize: new nation in Central America

By George C Price

Belizean Culture

The evolution of Belizean culture demonstrates a dynamic and ever-changing phenomenon, characterized by two distinct processes: suppression and cross-fertilization.

The African culture introduced into Belize by the slaves was systematically suppressed by the British slave-masters. The institution of slavery destroyed their political and economic systems, as well as their religion and family structure, although the slaves made great efforts to maintain and preserve as much of their culture as was possible under the circumstances. As recently as 1830 members of various African tribes in Belize still maintained some of their respective customs, among them the practice of each tribe choosing its own head. These attempts to uphold traditional systems were described by the British as "prejudices" and "superstitions." Those customs which were seen as threatening to the slave-masters, such as certain religious practices associated with revolt, were vigorously suppressed. Other cultural phenomena, however, such as music and dance, were largely treated with indifference.

Since the other ethnic groups were not at first completely integrated into the economy of the British settlers, their cultures were not as thoroughly suppressed. The Maya, for example, were able to maintain their ancient system of milpa farming and their language. They had already been exposed to Hispanization in that region and although their religion was suppressed, they managed to incorporate many of their ancient beliefs and rituals into the new religion and created their own interpretation of Christianity.

The phenomenon of co-existing cultures is very eveident among the Caribs of Belize, whose culture clearly exhibits features both of the cultures of Africa and that of the Caribs of the Eastern Caribbean. Though their language is largely derived from the island Caribs, their music and dance is clearly African.

Until recently, however, the dominant cultural influence on all groups has been British, since power was in the hands of the British, and British institutions, language, law, customs, values etc., were imposed.

Even so, the cross-fertilization process has, as far as it has been allowed, played a significant role in the development of Belizean culture. Wherever people of one culture co-exist along with people of other cultures within one organized, inter-dependent community, influences on each other develop, and the various cultures become common property, enriching each other.

As each group influences and is influenced by the others in a continuing dialectical process, new cultural manifestations occur to which all groups contrbute in a peculiarly Belizean context.

One such manifestation is the Belizean lingua franca (Belize Creole), an expressive idiom for the most part an adaptation and enrichment of English by

Afro-Belizeans, but with influences and word contributions by Caribs and Mestizos. The Spanish language, likewise, undergoes subtle transformation on the lips of the Spanish-speaking Belizeans, and is also influenced by Creole expressions, and, of course, when the Mestizo or Carib speaks "English," he speaks Creole.

Unfortunately, this cross-fertilization process was not allowed to develop freely in the colonial era. The colonial strategy of divide, sub-divide and rule ensured that, on the one hand, our various cultures remained largely isolated from each other and that, on the other hand, the colonizer's culture remained dominant. With the movement of liberation, however, the suppression of cultures no longer has a place in Belizean life, and the cross-fertilization process is now developing freely, enriching our Belizean culture, and reinforcing in the process a new and dynamic Belizean identity.

The character of Belizean cultural manifestations has been influenced by distinct internal and external factors. The chief internal influences were brought about by changes in the economic and political structure, while the external influences have come from our contact with the world outside.

From Belize:*New nation in Central America* by George C. Price. Benque Viejo del Carmen: Cubola Productions, pp. 6-7

Existing Conditions in the Field of Education: 1933/34

From B.H Easter

The provision of primary education was a joint Church/State partnership right from the beginning in 1816. By 1934 the denominational system where the different churches established and administered schools and the state provided the teachers salaries and other miscellaneous grants had been firmly entrenched.

Board of Education

The Churches were represented even at the highest level of Government machinery. At this level education was in the hands of a Board of Education which was an executive arm of the administration. The Board consisted of:

Governor ....President
Colonial Secretary..... Chairman (appointed by the Governor)
Members of the Executive Council
Five other members....usually General Managers of the different denominations.
Inspector of Schools.....Secretary

The Board had a life of three years and acted in an executive capacity. Its only limitations were (a) that funds had to be voted by the Legislative Council and (b) that its Rules must be approved by the Governor who was its President anyway.

Education Department

This board worked through the Education Department which was headed by an Inspector of Schools. The staff of the department consisted of:

1 Inspector of Schools—A Barrow Dillon
1 Assistant Inspector—V. H. Henry
1 Junior Clerk
1 Attendance Officer
1 Messenger

Dillon as secretary of the Board of Education was the liaison between the Board and the Managers and as Inspector he was the medium of communication between the Board and the teachers in the schools. The main function of the Inspector and his assistant was the individual examination of every child attending school above substandard.

Classification of Schools

For salary grants and staffing primary schools were classified as follows:
Class A—Schools (not being Infant Schools with an average attendance of 50 and upward. These schools were in Belize City or in the chief towns. In 1934 there were 21 Class A Schools.
Class C—Schools in Indian Villages. There were 17 Class C schools in 1934
Class B—All other schools. There were 37 Class B schools.

All schools were co-educational except two in Belize City—St. John's and Holy Redeemer. Belize City also had the only Infant School in the country.

Schools were organized in Infant and Primary classes. The statutory age was 5 to 16. The minimum average attendance for recognition as a grant-in-aid school was 15.

Salaries

Principal teachers were paid according to the type of certificate held and the class of school they were in. For example, a Principal teacher with a First Class Teachers' certificate in a Class A school would get $65.00 per month. One with a Third Class Certificate in a Class C school would get $25.00 per month.

Curriculum

In 1934 the curriculum was made up of :

1. Reading (History was a sub-division)
2. Writing (Letter-writing was a subdivision)
3. Arithmetic
4. Grammar
5. Geography (mostly map work)
6. Object Lessons—(These covered a fairly wide field of general knowledge: study of plants and animals, health, soil cultivation)
7. Needlework
8. Singing
9. School Gardening (in rare cases)

Textbooks

There was no uniformity in the use of textbooks in the schools. Furthermore, each child had to buy his own books. The readers in use were:
(i)   The Royal Readers
(ii)   West Indian Readers
(iii)   Granville Readers (R.C.Schools)
(iv)   Canadian Readers

Primary Schools

In 1932 there were 75 aided schools in operation with an enrollment of 8038 and an average attendance of 6585 or 81.92%. Of the 75 schools, 12 were in Belize City, 25 were in the district towns and the remaining 38 were in the rural areas. Education was compulsory and the ages for attendance were either 6 to 12 or 6 to 14.

The Pupil Teacher System was used to recruit local teachers.

Secondary Schools

There were four secondary schools in 1934 all situated in Belize City: St. John's College, (R.C.), St. Catherine's Academy (R.C.), St. George's College—(Anglican & Methodist), Diocesan High Schools for Girls (Anglican).

These schools received no financial aid from Government except what was earned as bonus by those schools whose pupils passed the Cambridge Local Examinations. The total enrollment for the 4 schools was only 158.

Emergency Measures 1933/34

Before the hurricane of 1931 teachers were paid according to a set salary scale. Besides the salary grants for teachers and pupil teachers Government paid to the different denominations a number of other grants. There were:

1. Attendance Grants—5 cents per month for each unit of average attendance.
2. Efficiency Grants—
    a. 25 cents, 45 cents, 60 cents, 75 cents (Infants 40 cents) according to passes in the respective standards at the annual examinations.
    b. 10 cents, 20 cents, 30 cents 40 cents according to % of passes
3. Pupil Teacher grants—$1.50 per month per Pupil Teacher to Principal Teachers for instructing Pupil Teachers.
4. Needlework, Agriculture, Industrial Subject Grants.

The Great Depression plus the hurricane caused a fall in Government revenue. Therefore, a number of emergency measures had to be introduced.

Among these were:

Deduction of 10% in official salaries
(i)   Reduction of 7% on all salary grants to teachers (this took effect in 1/9/32).
(ii)   Deduction of $1,000 for balance allocated for attendance grants
(iii)   Deduction of $1,950 allocated for Efficiency Grants
(iv)   Needlework grants were suspended as from 1/9/32
(v) $2,000 grant for building, equipment and furniture was abolished

Block Grant for Teachers' Salaries

The measure with most serious consequences for teachers was the substitution of Block Grants for the usual salary grants. The schedule of salaries for teachers and pupil teachers was suspended and the Block Grant did not provide full salaries of teachers. An immediate effect was a reduction in teachers' salaries. Furthermore, since salaries were no longer paid according to a fixed salary scale, the teachers' pay was entirely at the Manager's will. Another serious result was that Government, through Block Grants, exercised no control over the employment of qualified teachers.

Abolition of Formal Examination of Infants

The Board of Education Rules governing the payment of Efficiency Grants on Examination Results were amended in 1933 to abolish the formal examination of Infant Schools and Infant Departments. This was done to cut down the expenditure on efficiency grants which were paid on the results of such examinations. After this amendment only pupils in the primary classes were subjected to annual individual examinations.

Management

School managers of the various churches were members of the Board of Education. However, these were church officials primarily and Board members secondarily. Their loyalty was to their church but yet in the Board they acted as executives. The different managements worked independently of each other in all matters of school administration and organization. Church managers even supervised their schools to ensure that their sectarian positions were enhanced. Thus the schools were supervised by the Church and the Education department.

Population

The population was thinly scattered especially in the rural areas. Villages were not easily accessible and at certain times of the year almost inaccessible. Travel was slow and sometimes arduous. Thus rural schools were not only small and widely scattered but quite isolated. Available living accommodations in those villages were somewhat primitive.

Buildings

School buildings were owned by churches. A few, usually those in urban centres, were adequate and well-designed, but many of those in the rural areas were thatched houses and hardly adequate. Classroom equipment, material-aids and tools of teaching were also quite meager. Very often churches were used as schools.

Teachers

Teachers were selected by the school managers and paid by Government. Therefore teachers had two basic functions: teachers and catechists. Teachers in town schools usually had higher professional qualifications that those in rural areas. Weaker teachers tended to go into the smaller and more isolated schools. Principal teachers were often both teachers and trainers of Pupil Teachers.

Easter-Dixon Assessment of Prevailing Educational Situation

Teachers in the primary schools were mostly foreigners and many of them were untrained. Apparently, local personnel with adequate professional qualifications or potentiality for training were not available at the time. Most probably, however, the importation of teachers had resulted less form a desire to educate the children than from a desire to promote interests other than those of the children. Furthermore, teachers did not know whether their major responsibility was to the school manager or to the Superintendent. They were in the unhappy position of having dual responsibility: to the Church and to the State.

There was a marked absence of attractive classroom methods and the standard of attainment in the schools was generally low. Teachers in the rural areas did not make any serious attempt to relate the aims of the schools to the needs of the community. Efficiency of a school was assessed on the percentage of passes out of the total number of children presented for the annual examination. This method of assessment was most unsatisfactory.

Of major concern to both men was the duplication of efforts by denominational rivalry in the educational field. Very often two or more schools of different churches could be found in communities where there were hardly enough children for one school. Apparently, schools were established for the recruitment of future members of the individual denominations rather than for the education of the people.

No system of pension or retirement existed for teachers. Because of this, teachers continued in office long after the time when they had ceased to be fully efficient. Salaries were low and there was little opportunity for teachers to save for their old age.

Although there was provision for scholarships to secondary schools, no awards of such scholarships had been made to primary schools.

Dixon even observed that there was no national consciousness which could be found elsewhere. Although the country had been British since the 17th century there still existed a lack of that cohesion amongst the people which alone would weld them into a unified group.

From *The Easter and Dixon Reports* by I.E. Sánchez, M.A., B.Ed.. A.I.E. BISRA, No. 7. National Printers Limited: Belize, 1977, pp. 3-11

THE FOUNDATION OF THE SETTLEMENT: 1765-1817

Regulation of the Occupation of Land

The sole preoccupation of the early British adventurers was to export logwood, and they had no plan of establishing a permanent settlement in Belize. They built only temporary huts near the logwood groves, frequently changing their habitation to be near the logwood they were cutting. There was no regulation respecting ownership of land, each person cutting logwood wherever he might find it. This lack of any system of tenure was closely connected with the territory's legal status as the possession of another European colonial power, Spain. Before 1763, cutting operations frequently had to be abandoned as a result of Spanish attacks, but by Article 17 of the Treaty of Paris, signed on 10 February 1763, Great Britain obtained from Spain the right of British subjects to cut, load and carry away logwood unmolested in the Bay of Honduras. No definite boundaries within which the logwood cutters might operate were assigned. The Treaty emphasized that Spain retained sovereignty over the land, the British being given merely usufructuary rights limited to the exploitation of logwood. The original *raison d'etre* of the Settlement was therefore reinforced by Treaty, and this, together with the reservation of Spanish sovereignty, had far-reaching effects on the development of land tenure and land use in the Settlement.

In order to implement the terms of the Treaty, the British government in 1765 instructed Vice-Admiral Sir William Burnaby to visit the Settlement. During his stay, he attempted to bring some law and order to the Settlement, and in consultation with some settlers he drew up a set of primitive regulations, which became known as "Burnaby's Code." A rudimentary system of administration existed whereby the settlers gathered together in "Public Meeting" and passed "resolutions" which were deemed to have the force of law, and yearly elected magistrates who acted as semi-judicial officers. This system was given some rather vague recognition by Burnaby, without the authority of the Magistrates being clearly defined.

From *Land in Belize: 1765 -1871* by Nigel Boland and Assad Shoman. Institute of Social and Economic Research: University of the West Indies, Jamaica, 1977, p. 9

Tribute to a Mahogany Cutter

By J. Alexander Bennett

'Clare' he was to those who knew him well,
And even to the few to whom his worth
Was measured in the cubic feet of trees he fell—
To whom he was a labourer by birth.

And this man, Clare, faithful to his name
Was light unto that breed of toilers brave
Whose brawny arms brought tour country fame
And wealth-strong men who dreaded not the grave.

Unschooled, he was a teacher to the new
Woodsman who sought the secrets of his craft;
The art of cutting trees, known by so few;
The skill to ride the floods upon a raft.

They longed to know by what deep power he walked
Unhurt among leaf covered caves and lurking snakes;
With what dark ghost at early dawn he talked
Before he climbed his barbecue of stakes.

For all he had an answer; counsel wise:
"Be bold," he'd say, "observe, and be not blind.
Make sharp your wit; keep splinters from your eyes;
Love God, trust Him. He is your patron kind."

Unsung his name by those who do not know
How great the human cost of polished wood—
The toil, the grime, the pain, the flow
Of sweet. The countless drops must make a flood—

This woodsman true in life his country served,
To her he gave the labour of his hand.
For years, with unbowed head, purpose unserved,
He stood his ground while many left the land.

Today the paths he cuts among the woods
Are blocked once more by vine, and leaf and rust,
And Clare's name among discarded goods
In distant offices fast gathers dust.

But hewer though he was, let us recall—
He lived in the toil that we might freer be
To labour with our minds, give of our all,
Win for this land the gift of liberty.

From *Of Words: An Anthology of Belizean Poetry*, Cubola Productions: Benque
Viejo del Carmen, 1997, pp. 30-31

The Struggle Goes On

By E. Roy Cayetano

Africa,
Sixteenth century:
While I tilled African soil
for generations, centuries and millennia
intimately familiar with my footsteps,
digging stick, sweat and resting bones—
Land that gave me sustenance
and unites me here and now
with my yesterdays and tomorrows.
       The man came.
       The man took it all away.
       Agine was no longer mine
       Nor I Agine na.

St. Vincent,
Eighteenth century:
An all but lifeless thing
drifting in time and space, I,
And I chanced upon Yurumein,
A new beginning and a new set of footsteps
retraceable to the upper branches of the Amazon;
Africa grafted upon Amerindian Stock, I,
And I felt my roots grasp firm and deep
Yurumein soil whence drew, I,
life and a new tomorrow.

       The man came: I stood my ground.
       The man returned, and yet again.
       Satuye fell; and so did I.
       Yurumein was no longer mine
       Nor I Yurumein.

Belize,
Twentieth century:
Dragged and dispatched, defeated,
Dispossessed, undaunted spirit, I,
And I stumbled onto Belizean shore
amid stares from the many faces of the globe
including African brothers, American cousins,
My fellow victims of the man.
To this land of the Gods came I,

And I, with the optimism of Benein, the hope of Ramos,
My drum, cassava stick and fishing line,
Offered myself and my yesterdays to the new
Land of the Free-for all my tomorrows.
> The man is gone they say,
> With the despots, the tyrants.
> Can't you see his covetous eyes, plastered
> on faces staring at me and my land of the free?
> Balisi is my last stop, says I,
> And I and my tomorrows all Belisina.

From *Belizean Poets*, Part 3. Belize: Government Printers: Belize, 1972, p. 16-17

Excerpt from Labour Control In Post Abolition Belize

By O. Nigel Boland

The following account of the colony's system of labour control was published in 1883:

> The first principle in this system ......is the advance of three or more month's wages at the time of hiring. The labourer engages himself some time during the Christmas holidays for the ensuing year at say nine dollars per month. But he has just entered upon, or is in the height of, his few weeks annual festivity, and he and the woman he lives with, and the children, if any, require money "to keep Christmas." He applied for, and is granted four months' advance of wages; probably taking three to begin with, and spending it out, returning for another month's advance. But by his agreement he is bound to take half of his wages in goods from his employer, who keeps in his store a stock of such goods as his hands require, and of a certainly inferior quality. First of all, there is undue advantage on the employer's side...the evil of his (the labourer's) purchasing in the dearest market, instead of being allowed to take his money where he lives, is the lesser one only; the greater is that he receives these goods and the cash in the middle of a saturnalia of dissipation, and the consequences are the hard cash disappears like butter before the sun, finding its way into the tills of the rumsellers. The goods are next sold at one half what he is charged for them; that money, or the greater part of it also disappears, and another advance follows. The labourer has therefore to start his year's engagement three, four or even five months in debt. On the works the same rule of half goods half cast is pursued, but he sees no more cash although he gets goods. The bookkeeper of the gang keeps his account, debiting so much for every day he is absent from work, even for sickness, and exacting fines rigorously, the contract being in every way a tight one for the labourer. It is hardly necessary to add that when his season's work is over he finds himself in debt when he comes down to Belize for his Christmas spree. At no time is he capable of understanding his accounts clearly, and the time chosen for settling his year's accounts is when he is enjoying a continuous carousal...The system is a most pernicious one in every day. (Gibbs, 1883, 176-78).

The enforcement of this system of labour control depended on the District magistrates. Special Magistrates appointed during the "apprenticeship" period from 1834 to 1838 had dealt chiefly with complaints from the masters and there is no record of a complaint registered by an apprentice against a master. Since it is unlikely that the apprentices considered their masters' behaviour entirely beyond reproach, it is probable that they perceived the Special Magistrates as a disciplinary instrument of the masters (especially as the first two magistrates were local slave proprietors) to whom it would be pointless to address complaints. Certainly the Superintendent had stressed that the magistrates were to be primarily concerned with controlling the apprentices, with preventing "idleness, profligacy and insubordination," (Cockburn to Lefevre, 25 July 1834, CO 123/45) rather than with protecting them.

In 1849 the first paid district magistrate was appointed, and in the following year there were three magistrates in the Northern District, one in the Southern District, and on each in the Sibun and Belize river areas. In 1856 the payment of these district magistrates was regularized and the basis of the local administrative and judicial system was legally established. These district magistrates, like the Special Magistrates who preceded them, were to devote much of their energy to the enforcement of the Masters and Servants Acts. The magistrate at Corozal reported that all of the 286 cases decided by him under the colony's labour laws in 1869 consisted of discipline imposed upon the employees: 245 were punished for "absenting themselves from work without leave," 30 for "insolence and disobedience," 6 for "assaults on bookkeepers," and 5 for "entering into second contracts before the expiry of the period for former ones." (Adolphus to Longden, 15 Jan. 1870, AB, R. 105). Despite the criticism this magistrate included concerning the behaviour of the employers and particularly of the indebtedness caused by the advance and truck systems, he clearly functioned in his legal capacity as an instrument of discipline for the employers against the employed.

Under the colony's labour laws the magistrates could deal severely with the labourers who broke their contracts or were disobedient. One man, convicted of refusing to work and attempting to strike his employer, was fined one month's wages (eight dollars) and costs (two dollars), and another labourer, who hired himself to another employer before the expiration of his first contract, was sentenced to two months of hard labour in Belize jail. (Hamilton to Longden, 17 Feb 1870, AB, R. 106). In 1868 and 1869, 146 cases were brought by the "masters" against "servants" at the police court in Belize. Only one of these cases was dismissed; a common punishment among the others was three months' imprisonment with hard labour. In the same period ten cases were brought by "servants" against "masters," only one of these resulting in punishment, namely a two dollar fine. (Cockburn to Longden, 24 Feb. 1870, AB, R. 106). The severity of the sentences against employees and the paucity of cases against employers show that the labour laws and the magistrates who enforced them were operating in favour of the employers and were chiefly a means of disciplining and controlling the labour force.

From *Journal of Belizean Affairs*. Belize Institute for Social Research and Action. Belize: St. John's College, 9: 1979, pp. 28-30

Excerpt from The Labourer's Riot of 1894 (Conclusion)

By Peter Ashdown

[. . .] The prime target of the rioters among the merchants, Melhado of Cramer's, fled to the sanctuary of a ship in the harbour as his daughter reported that " The people are saying outside they want my father's life." At the height of the looting, around 4:45 PM, the Governor called Captain Macalister and a force of six officers and 85 men from the "Partridge" who quickly took over the guarding of strategic points (the Public Buildings, the Police Station, Government House and the Bridge) and accompanied the constables as they made arrests. Those arrests continued until the early hours of the next morning but the riot was really over once the "blue-jackets" had brought their discipline and guns to bear on the matter. The Governor, however, was taking no chances and cabled Downing Street that:

> Serious outbreak of labouring classes took place 11 December against employers. Slight loss of property, no lives lost, suppressed for the present by Partridge. Much agitation and great excitement prevails. Pelican arrived 12 December. Has been detained here. Application has been made for hundred and fifty (150) soldiers. Jamaica and HM ship "Canada" to be sent at once> consider that both absolutely necessary.

On the next morning rioters re-assembled and demanded the release of the twenty-two of their numbers arrested the day before. They threatened to break into the Police Station if this wish was not granted but made no effort to do so even when the ringleaders were marched from the Station to the goal after being remanded for a week, largely because a machine-gun escort had been brought in from the 'Partridge' and the D.C. had read the Riot Act. The ugly mood of the populace was, however, dissipated very quickly the same morning when the doyen of the merchant house, Bernard Cramer's, offered $10 gold and then $15 gold contracts which the other hiring firms agreed to match. This gave the lie to the merchants' former firm insistence that they could not improve on $7 and was undoubtedly brought on by panic as they realized that another 200 labourers had yet to descend on the capital for the Christmas festivities and hiring session.

Having placated their work force, in much the same way as the government had formerly pacified the mutineers, the merchants turned on the Governor whom they considered had been tardy in landing soldiers. They were quick to point out to Moloney that the riot act had started at 3:30 PM but that they had to defend their premises by themselves for an hour and a quarter with only the aid of a few constables. The merchants who had suffered losses claimed that the Administration was liable for the damages inflicted. The Governor refused to accept that he had been lax, insisting that if had landed troops prior to the rioting he would have been accused of being in league with the employers, noting that his job was "to hold the scale impartially between employers and employees and to avoid allowing the Government to appear to be favouring one or the other."

The Colonial Office, however, tended to agree with the Governor's detractors that he could have acted with greater alacrity but it was mainly concerned not with the riot's suppression but with its nature. It was relieved to note that the outburst was spontaneous and the result of coincidental adverse factors, and as such was relatively harmless and contrasted favourably with similar occurrences in the U.K., Ben Tillet and the 'dockers' tanner' loomed large in the Office's collective mind.

The fact that "the socialistic and adventurish element appear to be altogether wanting" was a relief, as was the absence of "red caps" and the "Marseillaise." It was considered that "Mr. Tom has the same qualifications as his English prototypes" but on the whole the Office was glad to note that the riot did not seem to be caused by any revolutionary ideology and, having established that, was not very concerned to censor the Governor, as it held no brief either for the merchants, whom it considered opportunist and self-seeking. It dismissed Cramer' claims and Melhado's "diatribes" noting that "this wily Portuguese renegade Jew" was seeking "to capitalize on the looting of his partner's store."

The culpability of the business oligarchy was also noted by the newspapers. The 'Times' while agreeing that the riot was shameful" felt that there was no denying that the labourers had grievances. It had earlier demonstrated that the forest workers' wages had fallen in real terms and that they were pawns in the hands of the employers as they had no organization to represent their interests. It concluded that there is no "blinking the fact that the Colony has been governed entirely in the interest of the mahogany and logwood merchants, and no attempt whatsoever has been made to develop its resources or to turn its natural advantages to account." The 'Colonial Guardian' too pointed out that the men had acted out of fear of starvation, but did not feel that the action which had "besmirched" the name of the Colony was in the circumstances justified. What concerned it most, as it had a month before, was not the rights or wrongs of the labourer's case but the vulnerability of law abiding citizens to "further outbursts of proletarian fury" as it reflected on the consequences of the riot had not a man-of-war been in the harbour.

The most immediate of those consequences was that of the trial of the rioters. Eventually 24 persons reached the dock but, of the 'ringleaders' only James McKoy was charged, the others having "fled to Bacalar." Of the 24 only six (McKoy, James Gibson, David Gregory, David Richardson, James Bartley and Robert Moloney) were convicted, the cases against the other eight being "not proven." Richardson, the assailant of McKenzie got nine months, but on the whole, the Constabulary and the Attorney General had failed rather dismally to demonstrate the penalties of disorder and the awfulness of the law.

[. . .] The riot, in fact, apart from a temporary increase in wages, achieved very little. It did, however, have several significant features which were to be important in future clashes between labour and capital in the Colony. Firstly, it was "unprecedented" there having been no such disturbance "in living memory" and probably not since the days of slavery. Secondly, in the words of the Governor, there was "abundant evidence to show the efforts of the rioters were solely directed against a limited number of employees of labour." It thereby contradicted the oft-repeated dictum that: hostility of race and class is peculiarly absent from British Honduras" for not only had it been an attack on exploitative capitalism (as represented by the merchant-employers) but it had also been partly a race riot. The Governor noted that his job, "to hold the scales impartially between employers and employees . . . and to allay . . . any friction between the two classes" had been made very difficult "when it is remembered that the distinction between employers and their employees is not limited to a distinction between labour and capital, but also embraces the distinction of colour." Molony considered that he had acted so that "all distinction between colour and class has been studiously avoided." This, however, did not stop such antagonisms manifesting themselves on the streets. The extent to which colour was a factor in the riot in the capital is debatable but it certainly was an important feature of a much smaller disturbance which took place in Stann Creek on December 15th. On that day 200 labourers of the British Honduras Syndicate in the Valley laid down their tools and 'went down' to the town where they forcibly closed down the Syndicate's store and threw lighted firecrackers through the District Commissioner's door. The Governor was forced to send a detachment of constables as it was reported that the men were angry with "an unknown grievance" and were threatening the Company's management and "white people in general." Frank Fisher (the British Honduras Syndicate manager) could report three months later to his superiors that "feeling is very strong in the race and colour question and even with the troops here now a white man is not safe from insult."

Racial friction was also to be a feature of the 1919 riot and, to a certain extent, important in the Soberanis troubles, but paramount in these outbursts and that of 1894 were class antagonisms. The 'Labourers Riot' had shown that all was not well in the relations between 'master' and 'servant' in the Colony. Far from being a classless society as Fred Gahne sometimes liked to pretend it was, British Honduras was socially deeply divided, so much so that after the Constabulary mutiny the 'Times' could say that "Had disorder occurred in the streets there is too much reason to fear that the Creole population generally would not have assisted the Europeans and the merchants." Gahne denounced this as " a gross libel on the Creoles of the Colony" but a fortnight later he was proven wrong. The 'advance' and 'truck' systems and the labour law may have forced labour into a state of complete dependency on the employers but, in the last analysis, that labour force had one recourse which only rifles and machine guns could repress. It was not to be the last time in Belize's history that the capital's employers and merchants had to be protected from their own employees.

From *Belizean Studies: A Journal of Social Research and Thought*. Belize Institute of Social Research and Action. St. John's College, Belize: 8: 1980, pp. 22-27

Excerpt from The Baymen's Legacy: A Portrait of Belize City

By Byron Foster

'A Slender Store of Tales'

A tradition dating back to remarks in the Honduras Almanack and the annals of Jamaica of 1827 derives the name Belize from 'Willis, the notorious Buccaneer...the first Englishman who settled on the banks of the river to which he gave his name. The Spaniards called it Wallis, and the corrupting influence of time has softened it to Belize;" the date of the settlement was given as 1638. A report of 1883 states that, " Peter Wallace, a Scotsman, landed with some eighty companions at the mouth of the Belize River and erected on its banks a few houses, which he enclosed with a rude palisade. His name was given both to the river and to the settlement." Wallace is also said to have been Sir Walter Raleigh's second-in-command and to have visited Belize before 1620[2].

'From this slender store of tales and suppositions,' comments a publication sponsored by the Colonial Office in 1968, 'have been concocted tales of piratical frays, which are as entertaining as they are improbable.'[3]

But what was regarded as improbable by the Colonial Office had in Belize become the basis of a whole ideology concerning rights ion the country. Hence when that ideology was challenged, a new derivation of the name Belize was suggested: an article in the Belize Times of 1958 claimed that the name derived from the Mayan term *belikin* (meaning 'towards the east'). This interpretation was appealing to Belizean nationalists since it 'signified their belief that the identity of the country is rooted in the ancestry of the indigenous Mayas of Central America,' rather than in British-oriented traditions.

Precisely because it asks the question, 'Who can legitimately claim the right to exercise hegemony over the people?' this debate is at the heart of Belizean life today. As long as the debate goes on-and it promise to be for a very long time-so the Belizean past will be a living part of its present.

The Buccaneer Settlement

Whether or not Captain Willis or Wallace ever settled at the river mouth, British buccaneers who had previously subsisted by privateering were cutting logwood at Campeche on the Yucatán Peninsula by the mid-seventeenth century, following the suppression of piracy. It is probable that Spanish harassment in the Yucatán led the cutters to move southwards; at any rate, a report to the British Council of Trade dated 1705 mentions the 'river of Bullys, where the English for the most part load their logwood.' Logwood was used in Europe to produce black, blue and purple dyes for use in the expanding textile industry, and the heartwood which yielded the dye was thus much in demand; Governor Modyford of Jamaica stated in 1670 that there were 'about a dozen logwood vessels formerly privateers, selling the wood at £25 and £50 a ton and making a great profit; and that they go to places uninhabited or inhabited only by Indians' and that 'if encouraged, the whole logwood trade will be English and be very considerable to His Majesty, paying £5 per ton custom.'[4]

The settlement at the Belize River mouth thus came into being for the purpose of exporting this valuable wood, which grows in stands near rivers and the coast. But what kind of society were the Baymen in the process of setting up? Captain Nathaniel Uring, who was shipwrecked off the coast of Belize in 1720 and who subsequently lived for several months amongst the cutters on the Belize River left us this account:

> In the dry Time of the Year the Logwood-Cutters search for a Work; that is, where there a good number of Logwood Trees; and then build a Hut near 'em, where they live during the Time they are cutting. When they have cut down the Tree, they Log it and Chip it, which is cutting off the Bark and Sap, and then lay it in Heaps, cutting away the Under-wood, and making Paths to each Heap, that when the Rain comes in which overflows the Ground, it serves as so many Creeks or Channels, where they go with small Canows or Dories and load 'em, which they bring to a Creek-side and lade their Canows, and carry it to the Barcadares, which they sometimes fetch Thirty miles, from whence the people who buy it fetch it. [...] The Wood-cutters are generally a rude drunken Crew, some of which have been Pirates, and most of them sailors; their chief Delight is in Drinking; and when they broach a Quarter cask or a Hogshead of Wine, they seldom stir from it while there is a Drop left: It is the same thing when they open a Hogshead of Bottle Ale or Cyder, keeping at it sometimes a Week together, drinking till they fall asleep; and as soon as they awake, at it again, without stirring off the Place. Rum punch is their general drink, which they'll sometimes sit several days at also; they do most Work when they have no strong Drink, for while the Liquor is moving they don't care to leave it. I had a very unpleasant Time living among these People...[5]

One God! One Aim! One Destiny! Marcus Garvey's Visit, 1921
Rally round the flag,
Rally round the red, gold, black and green.
Marcus say, Sir Marcus say,
Red for the blood that flowed like a river.
Marcus say, Sir Marcus say,
Green for the land, Africa.
Marcus say, yellow for the gold that they stole,
Marcus say, black for the people they loot it from...
In our hearts is Mount Zion,
Now you know, seek the lion...
Liberation, true democracy,
One God! One Aim! One Destiny!

Steel Pulse.

Marcus Mosiah Garvey, founder of the United Negro Improvement Association with its motto "One God! One Aim! One Destiny!" visited Belize City to rally the local branch of the U.N.I.A.

Born near St. Ann's bay, Jamaica, Garvey was 'perhaps the greatest of all Caribbean mass leaders.'[6] The aims of the U. N.I.A. are summed up in Garvey's own words: 'Where is the black man's government?' he wrote, 'Where is his King and his Kingdom? Where is his President, his country and his ambassador, his army, his navy, his men of big affairs?' 'I could not find them,' he continued, and then I declared ' " I will help to make them"... I saw before me then...a new world of black men, not peons, serfs, dogs and slaves, but a nation of sturdy men making their impress upon civilization and causing a new light to dawn upon the human race.'

The Belize City Branch of the United Negro Improvement Association had been opened in 1920 in the wake of the riot of 1919 which had protested the treatment of British Honduran servicemen during the First World War. Garvey addressed several meetings in Belize City complaining that 'Loyal blacks who had fought to protect the Empire had received in return only 'a kick and a smile" ', but taking care to stress the loyalty of the Association by ensuring that 'God save the King' was sung frequently by the assembled crowd. Garvey was particularly diplomatic in this respect for his newspaper, *The Negro World,* was regarded by the colonial authorities as seditious and on the 5th July he disarmed the governor at a meeting at Government House, stating that the U.N.I.A, stood for the uplift of negro people, 'morally, socially, educationally and industrially' and that 'In certain parts (the U.N.I.A.) stands for the liberty of the people, but where they are already free, such as in this Colony, we are doing our best to strengthen the moral life of the people.'

Garvey was heartily cheered at his public meetings in Belize City but his recruitment of the Belize branch's most capable member, Samuel Haynes, to the U.N.I.A. organization in the U.S.A. damaged the Association in the City; Garvey's reception on his second visit in 1929 was half-hearted, and not improved by its coincidence with the aviator Charles Lindbergh's visit to the Colony. The U.N.I.A., however, did succeed in coordinating the sentiments of the city's populace, helping to generate an awareness which was to be highly influential in subsequent years.

The Face of the City: Chronology

1638	Purported date of European settlement (unsubstantiated)
1705	Written record of presence of English logwood cutters on the 'River of Bullys.'
1787	Sketch map shows a court house and other buildings on the north side of the river mouth; the south side was divided into lots but separately unoccupied.
1792	James Dundas Yarborough, a magistrate, 'offered a piece of the plantation for a new cemetery.'
1803	A small fort, Fort George, erected on an island off the river mouth.

1810	South Side Canal begun as a twenty two foot wide drainage channel
1812	Construction of St. John's Cathedral
1818	Court House constructed on South side
1820	Market and slaughter house built, probably on the site of an earlier market on the South side
1827	Gaol completed, close to what is now the junction of Church Street and Albert Street
1829	New canal opened; the old canal was probably Richard's Canal, which has been converted into a street
1863	Back Street became Albert Street
1900	Pound Yard established to keep the Town free of stray dogs
1903	First motor car imported
1912	Royal Bank of Canada opens branch in the Town
1918	Court House burned down
1919	Collet Canal completed. Mesopotamia laid out and settled, 1919-1928
1920	Central Police Station established (Eastern Division)
1923	Swing Bridge opened. Reclamation begun, to form Fort George area.
1926	Baron Bliss tomb and lighthouse constructed. New Court House and administration buildings erected.
1933	B .E.C. sawmill constructed on North Side
1943	Belize Town becomes Belize City
1945	Suction dredge used to fill areas known as Cinderella Town, King's Park and Caribbean Shores. Queen's Square district expanding form Collet Canal in late 1940's, early 1950's
1949	Barclays Bank established
1950	Construction of St. John's College began
1964	Radio Belize begins broadcasting from Albert Cattouse building
1965	Prisoner Creek Area becomes Lake Independence
1969	Belcan Bridge opened
1970	Government departments transferred to Belmopan

From *The Baymen's Legacy: A Portrait of Belize City* Belize: Cubola productions (1987), pp. 11-13, 59-60, 80

A September Morn Long Ago

By Dr. Henry Anderson

The sun had laboured and come up
That long ago September morn;
With passing clouds it still was hot,
Each Bayman slumbered on his cot.
The flies were circling round and round
And sweat was dropping on the ground.
A little drizzle touched the roof;
An ugly cloud passed far aloof.
It was about mid-morning time
In this hot of hottest clime;
All the Baymen did was nap
Upon His Royal Highness cot.

The Magistrate was terribly worried,
So he and the Sergeant rather hurried,
Stretched their legs towards the sea.
A ship or two they looked to see,
But not a speck till blue met blue
Just clouds and surf if sight held true.

St. George's Caye! St. George's Caye!
Home of the Baymen, you and me!
From this land we will never flee.
St. George's Caye! St. George's Caye!
Many times have the Spanish come,
Many times have they had to run.
So, while the Baymen on the King's cot,
He keeps his musket piping hot.

As muskest not for all around
Some sit with sticks upon the ground.
Sticks, form the coconut boy tree,
Prickled and sharpened weapons they be.
Brought from the mainland to the caye;
Brought in doreys across the sea.
Such prickles, long and straight and strong,
Across the backs of those who wrong.
Surely, did the Spaniards know of this
St. George's Caye he'd definitely miss.

As I had mentioned to you before,
The Magistrate and the Sergeant on the shore
Did search and search to see some form
This drizzly and darkening September morn.
Then suddenly with step astride
The glass was swiftly swung aside.
"A ship! A ship! I see a ship!
It comes to us at a very fast clip.
Is it ours? Is it not?
Oh my goodness, this is hot."

The Magistrate did then spy
To see the ship come bye and bye.
No flag could he discern at first.
His throat was dry: a sudden thirst.
Then in a hurry things got hot,
Cooks forgot their fire and pot.
The church bell rang and the cannon rolled.
The Baymen form their homes did pour
And marching bravely up and down
Their muskets fired out a round.
And held up high the Baymen's sticks
Nothing sharper than those pricks.
Boom! Boom! Boom! Did the Baymen hear,
And cannon balls were in the air.
The ship afar out at sea
Was a decoy between you and me,
For suddenly from around a mangrove patch
Some Spaniard ships sailed for their catch;
And never in our history before
Was Spaniard ship so close to my shore.
Spaniard warships numerous at hand
Only Baymen doreys to protect our land.

The Spaniards knew of our mahogany stock
But they hadn't charted our coral rock.
They came like rats fleeing out a hole
But in the daylight were the moles.
Booming booms from left to right
The Spaniards rallied for the fight.
But God for us that September day,
A swift breeze rose upon the Bay.
Some said it was a hurricane, I don't know,
It sent the ships upon the shoal

Where the winds and waves battered, here and there,
While cannon balls and coconuts filled the air.

When the Pork-and-Dough Boys began the attack;
Many ships collapsed upon coral rocks.
Amidst the Spaniards confusion spread
And musket lead soon dropped them dead.
But the Baymen did not put all in Hell,
For some had to go back, the story to tell.
And as the prickles they took from their backs
They swore that to Belize they'd never come back.
And, so my friends, as I end this tale,
Of that September morn, the battle and the gale,
I hope you'll remember the Baymen's fight;
To be in our history, forever a right,
For they were the ones who saved this land,
Given to us by God's own hand.

From *The Son of Kinich* by Dr. Henry Anderson: Jaribu Books, Dangriga (1995), pp. 129-132

Excerpt from <u>Slavery in Belize</u>

By O. Nigel Bolland

The Slave Population

Origins
   The slaves who were brought to the Bay of Honduras were imported through the West Indian Islands. One early 19th century account stated that "these have been mostly imported from Africa by the intercourse with Jamaica, no direct importation having ever taken place; but many of these people are Creoles of the different West Indian Islands, and several have been brought into the Settlement, by their owners, from the United States."[7] Later, it was stated that they were " imported from Africa, either direct or through the West India islands."[8] Though there is no indication from the 18th century records of the proportion of the slaves who were of African as opposed to West Indian birth, in 1823 it was estimated that there were in Belize "near 1500 Africans" in a slave population of about 2300, "the remainder being Creoles and descendants of the Indians"[9] the latter from the Mosquito Shore. If it is correct that about three-fifths of the slaves were African-born in 1823 it can be safely assumed that the Creoles were always a minority of the slaves.
   Additional to the distinction between African-born and Creole slaves was the difference in the tribal origins of the African-born slaves. Because these slaves were brought through island slave markets there are no shipping records to indicate their tribal identity but the names of many of the slaves recorded in a 1790 census indicate a variety of national origins, for example such names as Congo Will, Angola Will, Guinea Sam, Eboe Jack, Mangola Sam, Mundingo Pope and Corromontee Tom. Most of the slaves were brought to the Bay Settlement in the second half of the 18th century, at which time the principal source of the British slaves were the Niger and Cross deltas in the Bight of Benin (from 1730 to 1790) and Southwestern Africa, particularly the Congo and Angola (from 1790 to 1807).
   The Eboes or Ibos appear to have been particularly numerous in Belize. One section of Belize Town was known throughout the first half of the 19th century as Eboe Town and was said to consist of "numerous yards, flanked with long rows of what are called negro houses, being simply separate rooms under one long roof, which used to be appropriated to slaves, and now accommodate the poorer labourers."[10] In 1850 it was stated that there were in Belize "Congoes, Nangoes, Mongolas, Ashantees, Eboes and other African tribes"[11], indicating that tribal distinctions and identifications persisted well after emancipation.

Demographic Features

One of the major factors affecting master/slave relations in Belize was the overwhelming numerical preponderance of the blacks, more similar to Jamaica than to Barbados or the North American colonies. Before the middle of the 18th century the slaves were the majority of the population and at the time the Spaniards captured the settlement in 1779 there were an estimated three thousand slaves in the bay or about 86 percent of the total population. After the resettlement following the peace of 1783 about 75 percent of the population were slaves, 14 percent were free blacks and "coloured," and about 10 percent were white. With the development of the demand for mahogany the settlement expanded again and hundreds more slaves were imported prior to the abolition of the slave trade in 1807. Following the abolition of the trade, the number of slaves in the settlement decreased from about three thousand to under two thousand at the time of emancipation. During this quarter century the proportion of the slaves also declined dramatically from about three-quarters to less than half of the population, while the free black and coloured increased from about one quarter to almost a half and whites remained about one tenth of the population.

TABLE 1—Slave Population of Belize 1745-1832 [12]
Number of Slaves

Date	Male	Female	Children	Total	Slaves as Percentage of Total Population
1745	....	....	....	120	71
1779	....	....	....	3,000	86
1790a	1,216	550	411	2,177	75
1790b	1,091	515	418	2,024	76
1803	1,700	675	584	2,959	75
1806	1,489	588	450	2,527	72
1809	....	....	....	3,000	73
1816	....	....	....	2,742	72
1820	1,537	600	426	2,563	....
1823	1,440	628	400	2,468	60
1826	1,373	577	460	2,410	46
1829	1,113	486	428	2,027	52
1832	895	435	453	1,783	42

The slaves in Belize were unable to reproduce themselves. There was probably a high rate of mortality resulting from such factors as diseases, malnutrition, ill-treatment and overwork and the slaves sometimes killed themselves. Moreover, the rate of reproduction was very low, partly because of a severe imbalance of the sexes (generally two or three men to every woman) and because of the practice of abortion, said to be "extremely common" and having "its avowed professors" among the slave women[13]

The slave population was also a relatively old population, the proportion of slaves who were under ten years of age generally being about 17 percent in the 1820's while the proportion of the slaves who were forty years old or more increased from about one fifth in 1820 to about one third in 1834. However, the fact that, at this latter date, men outnumbered women by only seven to six under the age of forty, compared to ten to three at age forty years or more, suggests at least a potential for greater demographic stability in the slave population shortly before emancipation.

So long as slaves could be imported to Belize their numbers increased, but with the abolition of the slave trade the number of slaves, and their proportion to the rest of the population, declined dramatically. This decline was due in part, to high mortality rates but also to a variety of factors which kept birth rates low. In addition, one must consider the relatively high incidence of manumission and the large numbers of slaves who escaped from the settlement. However, even when it is taken into account that about six hundred slaves were manumitted and about two hundred escaped between 1807 and 1834, it is apparent that the slave population was not able to reproduce itself. Even if these eight hundred people had remained in slavery, there would have been fewer slaves in 1834 than there were in 1807 because of a natural decrease in population.

The fact that in 1834, 26 per cent of the slaves were aged forty years or more is a reflection of the great importation of young male slaves in the years immediately preceding the abolition of the slave trade. This emphasis on young men in turn reflected the nature of the labour demands in an economy that was devoted almost exclusively to the arduous tasks of mahogany extraction.

From BISRA Occasional Publication #7, "Slavery in Belize" by Nigel Bolland, (Belize, 1979), pp. 5-8

Chapter 4

Myths and Legends

La LLorona

"Woe on him whom she seduces with her beauty and who having compassion on her weeping draws near to console her."

The story is told of a wealthy landowner who went on business trips which kept him away from his wife for long periods of time. His wife often became restless and, during one of his absences, had an illicit affair. As a result, she bore a child. Knowing that she would not be able to convince her husband that the baby was his, she went to the river and drowned the child. The legend of LA LLORONA, whose name is Spanish for "the weeping woman," tells that this woman has been cursed by God since then and now she sits disconsolately on a rock by a river or creek combing her long, wavy black hair and crying pitifully, hoping to inspire the mercy of those who hear her.

Stories of LA LLORONA are popular in Belize, especially in the district of Orange Walk, and also in the neighboring countries of Mexico and Guatemala. Although LA LLORONA and XTABAI have traditionally become merged into one legend and, as enchantresses, are said to be variations of the same lore, each possesses distinct characteristics and behaviour.

Though seen most often near the water, LA LLORONA can also be found inland, at the roadside or under an almond or a breadfruit tree. On dark, lonely nights, her haunting cries and her appearance of helplessness give her an alluring charm which draws men to her. She also attracts a man's attention by allowing fire or a glowing light to come from her fingers, and as the man gets nearer, LA LLORONA appears to float in the air, moving farther and farther away as the man follows her. Men who encounter her at midnight near rivers, or at crossroads, may witness her turning into a two-tailed serpent. She then sticks her tails into the victim's nostrils and squeezes. Travelers or drunks who have lost their way can become her unfortunate victims, and their greatest fear is to be wrapped in her thick, long hair and taken over the water to a region from where no one can return.

Late one evening, Don José and his assistant were coming from a distant village on horseback. They rode along the riverside at a steady pace, until Don José, who was at the front, came to a sudden stop. His gaze had fallen on a remarkably beautiful woman who sat at the river's edge, wailing miserably. He was irresistibly drawn to her and dismounted, instructing his assistant to wait for him. He walked eagerly toward the woman, and as soon as she saw him, she beckoned to him to follow her. She led the way for a while, and Don José followed her eagerly. The curious assistant had been following them discretely and suddenly heard his employer scream, "¡Cuidado!" The seductress was heading towards a dangerous curve in the river, where the current raged. The assistant watched as his employer approached the woman to try to save her. As he embraced her, she enveloped him in her long hair, and they both disappeared into the water. The assistant returned home in a state of shock and many days later told how his employer had been carried away by the weeping woman.

From *Characters and Caricatures in Belizean Folklore*. Belize:UNESCO Project(1991) pp. 35-36

Excerpt from Old Benque

Por David N. Ruiz Puga

Los Finados

[. . .] Sacaron cinco tazas con nance curtido y cinco con conserva de ayote que doña Chepona había preparado días antes. Después pegaron las velas alrededor de la mesa. Doña Tencha fue al fogón y cogió un puñado de cenizas y lo regó alrededor de la mesa en donde había colocado todos los dulces; y, con las velas encendidas, comenzaron el novenario a las almas benditas del purgatorio.

Al paso del tiempo y con el rezo monótono, el niñito se fue durmiendo. Enriqueta lo comenzó a arrullar, se levantó de la banqueta y le dijo a doña Chepona:

_ ¿Puedo acostar al niño?

_ ¿Ya se durmió?

_ Sí

_ Pues, vamos. Pero no vayas a dejarlo solo.

_ ¡Ay no doña Chepa!

Las dos mujeres se dirigieron al cuarto y encendieron la lámpara que estaba en la mesita. Claudio Homero estaba bien envuelto en ropas y cobijas blancas.

_Cuando llegue la hora lo despierto—dijo la madre.

En eso se oyeron las primeras gotas de agua que caían sobre la cubierta de guano.

_¡Ave María Purísima!—exclamó doña Chepona tronando los dedos—Ya empieza la llovizna. _¡Enriqueta, ya se acerca la hora!

_ Cálmese doña Chepona. Aquí estamos nosotros. Vaya con los demás; yo me quedo con el niño. Vaya uste', que con la oración nada le puede pasar.

Doña Chepona se unió al rezo. Para entonces ya eran las once y media de la noche. La llovizna parecía más fuerte y el aire silbaba dentro de los matorrales. Hacía ratos que se había dejado de oír el griterío de los niños con sus calaveras. Al terminar de rezar, todos quedaron viéndose unos a otros. Solamente se oía el viento que soplaba trayendo consigo la incesante llovizna. Doña Chepona comenzó a pasearse por toda la casa. Se frotaba las manos y miraba a todos con profunda angustia.

_Perdone, comadrita—dijo don Cornelio después de un rato—, pero yo no he podido concentrarme en el rezo ya que tengo curiosidad de ver el hueso que uste' dice.

Al oír a don Cornelio hablar, todos murmuraron:

_ Es cierto, déjenos ver el hueso.

_ ¡Ah! ¡Sí!_ contestó doña Chepona nerviosa_. Ya la hora está más cerca, voy por él.

Entró a su cuarto calladamente y abrió el cofre. Metió la mano y levantó la toalla en la que había envuelto el hueso. Enriqueta se había recostado cerca del niño y, al oír entrar a doña Chepona, se levantó y salió junto con ella. Doña Chepona se dirigió hacia la mesa donde estaban las conservas y comenzó a abrir el bulto. Todos se amontonaron curiosamente alrededor de ella y suspiraron al ver lo que ésta había desenvuelto.

_ ¡Ay! ¡No—gritó doña Chepona tirándose en brazos de doña Tencha. Comenzó a gritar histéricamente mientras se aferraba a la señora. Y entre los gritos de desesperación, se oyó la voz temblorosa de doña Candelaria.

—¡Sí es una vela!—

_Nunca había visto una tan galana—dijo don Cornelio levantando la vela. Y a como la vela pasaba de mano en mano todos la escudriñaban como si estuvieran observando algo de otro mundo.

—Bueno, y que…

Doña Candelaria estaba por preguntar lo que todos deseaban saber, pero fue precisamente en esos momentos cuando se oyó el chirriar de los portones de la iglesia.

—¿Oyeron eso?—preguntó don Cornelio sin pestañar.

—¡Ya vienen! ¡Ya vienen!—gritó doña Chepona levantándose del banco donde la había sentado doña Tencha. Doña Chepona estaba en un solo temblor y miraba horrorizada hacia la ventana. Don Cornelio la abrazó y mandó a doña Candelaria a hacer un poco de café.

—Comadre-dijo firmemente-Uste' tiene que ser muy fuerte. Contrólese. Haga lo que le dijo el Padre Arturo y todo va a salir bien. Aquí estamos todos nosotros, y vamos a ayudarle.

Doña Chepona apretó los ojos y tartamudeó.

—Sí…com…compadre. Voy …voy a ha…hacer…m…mi parte.

Todos formaron un círculo alrededor de doña Chepona y esperaron. Doña Candelaria llegó enseguida con el café y le dio de beber a doña Chepona quien ya se veía un poco más tranquila. Enriqueta sacó al niño del cuarto y lo despertó. El niño comenzó a llorar y Enriqueta empezó a amamantarlo, mientras hacía todo lo posible para mantenerlo despierto.

Esperaron un rato y nada. Todos estaban angustiados. Don Cornelio empezó a pasearse e inconscientemente entró a la cocina. Y, al ver que estaba en el sitio por donde su comadre había visto la procesión, no resistió la tentación de espiar. Vio claramente como la neblina flotaba en los alrededores. La llovizna no estaba tan fuerte como creía. Dirigió su mirada a la iglesia en la cual reinaba un profundo silencio. Estaba a punto de levantarse cuando se oyó el ruido de las puertas que parecían abrirse. Y don Cornelio no pudo creer lo que veía. Observó como las figuras altas y blancas bajaban en procesión con sus velas encendidas. Don Cornelio no pudo más. Sintió un peso en el cuerpo y apretó los ojos. Luego se levantó agarrándose de un lado de la mesa y trastabilló hacia adentro.

Para eso, las señoras se habían juntado en una esquina del cuarto rezando el rosario. El eco del melancólico canto llegaba a todos los rincones. Doña Chepona parecía haber recobrado ya sus fuerzas. Cargaba al niñito en brazos mientras que Enriqueta, toda temblorosa, trataba de ponerle la vela en la mano izquierda, sin ningún éxito. Trató de varias maneras para que el niño agarrara la vela pero éste no la podía sostener.

—Es imposible-dijo don Cornelio—, la vela está demasiada pesada para él.

—¡Apúrense, que ya vienen!—vociferó doña Chepona.

Se podía notar que escondía un profundo terror.

—¡Ya sé que hacer!—exclamó don Cornelio triunfante. Corrió a la ventana y la entreabrió.

—¡Comadre!—ordenó—¡Traiga al niño!—

Para eso, Claudia Homero pegaba de gritos.

—¡La vela! ¡La vela! ¡Enriqueta!—gritó don Cornelio—Tenemos que calmar al niño. Enriqueta, tómalo.

La madre tomó al niño y lo comenzó a arrullar. Para entonces, ya se oía el canto cercano de la muchedumbre.

—No se distraigan-dijo don Cornelio a las mujeres que se habían detenido a mitad del Rosario, atemorizadas por tan extraño suceso.—¡Sigan rezando! ¡No se detengan!

[. . .] La procesión ya pasaba por la casa. El aire frío que entraba por la ventana invadía todo el cuarto. Doña Chepona cargó al niño y se agachó. Luego, siguiendo las instrucciones de su compadre se aseguró que el niño estuviera completamente cubierto excepto las manitas y lo subió hasta la ventana. Don Cornelio, por otro lado, también se aseguró de que el bebé estuviera a la altura del sillar de la ventana. Luego, dejó que el niño apretara una punta de la vela mientras que el otro extremo se soportaba en el sillar. Mientras hacía esto, don Cornelio trató de no mirar directamente hacia el callejón. Pero aún así, no pudo evitar ver las figuras borrosas en procesión. Luego, corrió hacia las mujeres que seguían rezando con ojos cerrados la letanía de Todos los Santos.

Doña Chepona sentía que había estado horas sosteniendo al niño en lo alto de la ventana. Temblaba y ya sentía que el cansancio y la desesperación la empezaban a invadir.

—Dios mío. ¡Que pase esto lo más rápido posible!—

De pronto, sintió que el niño se movía.

—Dios Santo. Si sigue así va a tirar la vela-pensó mordiéndose los labios de aflicción.

Y luego, sintió una fuerza que trataba de arrancarle al niño de sus manos. Le dieron ganas de levantarse a ver que pasaba pero sabía perfectamente bien que no debía hacerlo; aún tenía muy presente el suceso de la noche anterior y la advertencia del Padre Arturo.

Nuevamente, sintió que alguien tiraba del niño, y esta vez más fuerte. Doña Chepona, ya con los brazos entumecidos, sacó todas sus fuerzas par agarrar fuertemente al niño quien comenzaba a llorar. Y al sentir una presencia muy cerca de ella, cerró los ojos. De pronto una voz de ultratumba vibró por los aires y se escuchó decir:

—¡Que te valga mujer!—

From *Old Benque* by David N. Ruiz Puga (Cubola Productions: Benque Viejo del Carmen), 1990, pp. 149-156

The Black Goat Speaks

By Nicholas A. Pollard Sr.

'Twas the poet Tennyson, I think, who said:
"For what are men better than sheep or goats
That nourish a blind life within the brain,
    If knowing God, they lift not hands of prayer
        Both for themselves and those who call them friend.?"

'Twas in the dry and dusty month of May
When all devoted people wend their way
    To Church, there Mary, Heaven's Queen, to praise:
        "Hail Mary, full of grace, thou art among thy children fair
        Lily of eternal choice!"

As thus they praised ('twas in Castillian pure),
    Not more than fifty strong, they were I'm sure;
    In front of all a brother* knelt in prayer
    When upon a pew in front so empty, bare,
        Arose a thing—methought it was Satan—
        So black, so black it was
            It was—a goat!

Straight at the brother's face he stared,
    Then at the fifty strong in turn.
    So black, so mute, so dumb he looked,
        Our voices must needs become hushed somewhat,
        Our faces red and round with stifled smiles—
        Placed there by God or devil's wiles
            I cannot tell.
                But gazed and blinked and gazed
                    Without a word.

Then to my shocked brain the sermon came:
    "Must I a goat, and dumb to wit,
        Here sit
            In place of men who do not care to pray,
                Who do not know of Mary's month of May?"

My smile I ceased—
    The goat had disappeared . . .

But—was there wiser creature upon earth
  Than a Black Goat of our Redeemer Church?

*The brother referred to here was Br. John Mark Jacoby S. J., O.B.E., late great
founder of the Boy Scout Movement in Belize.

From *Belizean Poets, Part 3*, Government Printers, Belize (67)

Excerpt from My Uncle Ben

By Zoila Ellis

[. . .] As I sat on the bench watching the lovers and thinking, something happened inside and everybody rushed to the doors and windows to look. I went but could see nothing because of the crowd. Suddenly, the crowd at the door ran screaming and laughing as someone staggered out. I thought he was sick first, because he was flinging his hands in the air and moving jerkily. Then he flung himself on the ground and began writhing in the sand. He tore off his shirt and began dancing on his bottom as strange sounds came form his mouth. I was surprised to see the crowd laughing and then a woman said, "Look he Oweha! Oweha!" Then I understood what was happening. According to Ma, when a person was like that, the spirit entered his body and made it do things the person would never remember afterwards. Something made me look at the man closely and when I saw it was Uncle Ben, I ran towards him but a woman pulled me back.

"Leave him alone," she said "or the spirit will be angry wid you."

I started to cry and ran inside to find ma. The crowd was thick and I did not find her for a long time. When she saw me weeping she pulled herself outside the crowd, demanding to know what was wrong. I told her and to my surprise she burst into laughter. By the time she stopped laughing she was gone. I rushed outside only to discover that Uncle Ben had also gone. His shirt was on the ground where he must have torn it off.

[. . .] Next morning Uncle Ben did not appear for tea at six. This was strange because if he could help it, Uncle Ben never missed his cassava bread and fish. We all thought he was still shocked over last night's episode so we were not worried. Ma sniffed and said he would soon show up if she knew him. Well, she did not know him because he didn't come. Not for dinner at twelve, not for tea at six that night either. I felt sorry for him and asked Pa to go and look for him, but Pa had a headache and was too tired to go out.

That night I dreamt that Uncle Ben was floating down to the bottom of the sea and the fishes were nibbling on his fingers and toes. I heard him calling my name and when I reached out to grab him, he moved further and further away. Finally, I managed to grab one of his fingers and started pulling him to get him out of the water. I squeezed his fingers tighter and tighter and he seemed to be pulling away from me.

[. . .]

The next morning pa set out early with seven men with doreys and headed east. They left form the pier after searching the beach form the beginning of the town to the end. [. . .] That day no one was happy and everyone was wondering what was happening to Uncle Ben.

[. . .] All my aunts came to visit us that morning and all they talked about was Uncle Ben, the *Dugu* and what could have happened to him.

[. . .] At six in the evening, father Delaware, the wrinkled white priest, came in a long gown faded to the colour of his skin. He carried a Bible in his hand and proceeded to lead the Rosary. Everyone gathered in a circle and prayed and prayed until I thought they would never stop. Father would say a long prayer and they would answer a short sentence in Latin. We all stood with our heads bowed, but I could not pray a word.

[. . .] I wondered if Uncle Ben was cold where he was and if God could understand Latin, or if Carib was too cheap a language in which to ask him if could please drop a blanket and bread from the sky like he did for those people in the desert. [. . .] I sat down on a chair and slept.

I was awakened by voices outside, one of which sounded like Pa's, and I jumped up. All eyes turned to the door as it was opened by Joe Melendrez followed by Pa. Some men behind came in carrying Uncle Ben.

"The Lord has answered our prayers," I heard Father Delaware saying, beginning another prayer. I could not pay attention for I was watching Uncle Ben.

His trousers were torn and he was soaking wet.

Ma screamed and rushed to him crying loudly.

"Nugushi! Nugushi!."

[. . .] He was trembling like he had chills and she rubbed his forehead with bay rum and *ruda*. After that, she [Ma] covered him with a thick blanket.

All the next day and the day after that, Uncle Ben would not eat or drink. [. . .] All had heard about the *Dugu* and advised ma to have the *Buye* visit him since it was clear that he had angered the spirit and was being punished. [. . .]

That evening the Buye came. She spent three hours in his room. None of us children were allowed in the house whilst she was there. [. . .] I could not imagine what she was doing. Father Delaware called her a devil worshipper. Ma, Aunt Candelaria and all my mother's relatives believed in her powers and said she healed the sick. I did not think that to heal the sick was bad, but I did not understand why Pa disliked her the way he did.

Was something wrong with the drums and the music and the things that we did at the Temple? Which spirits had punished Uncle Ben because he did not believe? I could not understand any of it and there was no one I could ask except Uncle Ben, and now he was dying.

Before the *Buye* came out of the room I knew Uncle Ben was dying. I listened to Ma and my aunts wailing loudly in the yard as the *Buye* told them that Uncle Ben would die in two days.

I called Christina, Joseph, Bernadette and all my other brothers and sisters around me, and told them that Uncle Ben was going to die. They looked solemn and Joseph started to sniff.

"Don't worry," I promised. "I will tell you stories now. I will take you for walks on the beach to pick up shells and go fishing on the pier and everything." They nodded, saying nothing . . .

From *On Heroes, Lizards and Passion* by Zoila Ellis. (Belize: Cubola Productions, 1988) 33-37.

La Sirena

"When she lures you, she takes you to the lonely road where she leaves for lost all those who fall under her spell."

A weeping spirit associated with water and streams, LA SIRENA, has long, black hair and is fully clothed in white. Stories of LA SIGUABANA in some Belizean communities indicate that she is the same character as LA SIRENA. The word SIRENA translates literally from the Spanish as "mermaid," whose half-woman, half-fish body is comparable to the half-woman, half-snake body of LA SIRENA. Her face, which may sometimes be hidden, is described by some as beautiful and by others as ugly. Some versions even say she is hiding a horse's face or a skull underneath the cloth she wears over her head.

LA SIRENA is believed to be the spirit of an evil woman who grew tired of her child and threw it into a stream to drown. She now sits near the river at night, and many people fear seeing her, for it may be an omen of their death. She will sometimes carry children off for three days, and when she returns them, they are disoriented and unable to function normally for several days. Most often, however, she chooses men who are roaming late at night, especially drunks, as her victims. She impersonates men's sweethearts and leads them down a path from which it is difficulty to return, and those who search for a way out become frustrated and delirious.

One Maya legend about LA SIRENA tells that she was created by the supreme evil being from objects in the environment. When he was ready to put hair on her, his eyes rested on a nearby tree and he used its branches to form her hair. The following story is often attached to this legend.

A young villager had been drinking with his friends all day and was returning home on horseback. His journey took him through some forested areas, and in one such area, an attractive woman suddenly appeared before him. He dismounted in order to approach her, and as he came nearer, she tried to embrace him. He then realized that she was the enchantress LA SIRENA spoken of in his village, but he was under her spell already and was being compelled to follow her. He tried to stop himself from going further by grabbing onto the branches of a tree and was immediately released from her spell. The tree he had held on to was the same one used to make LA SIRENA'S hair, and legend has it that pulling on the branches of the tree makes her feel as if someone is pulling her hair.

Among the Garinagu, stories are told of the AGAYUMA, who resides near the water, and seduces men with her long, silken hair and her shapely body, whose form she can change to resemble various water creatures. AGAYUMA's victims are plagued by dreams of her, and only a special item given them by the *buye* or medicine man will keep the dreams away. If, however, no precautions are taken, the victims waste away and die.

Some years ago, in the village of Barranco, five girls told of their encounter with the AGAYUMA during the dry season. They had all gone to fetch water from the pond, and while there, they saw an apparition which each reported as a fair woman, dressed in full white. She sat near the edge of the pond, from where she rose floating toward the bush, disappearing into the trees. They thought they had seen the Blessed Virgin Mary, but the elders of the village heard the story and concluded that the girls had, in fact, seen the AGAYUMA.

MAMA DLO or MAMA DGLO, derived from the French "maman de l'eau," meaning mother of the water, is a Caribbean character who bears close resemblance to our SIRENA. Her lower body is coiled like a snake, and although her facial features are repulsive, she can take the form of a beautiful woman, singing softly near the water's edge.

From *Characters and Caricatures in Belizean Folklore* (Belize: Belize UNESCO Commission, 1991), 25-26

One Day in the Plantation with Tata Duende

By Dr. Henry B. Anderson

Da mi di merry month of May;
Da mi wa hat and summer day;
Di leaves mi green;
Di fruits mi red;
Di bees midi dance like dey dead;
Di river bed mi nearly dry
Like Dangriga's water supply;
Di squirrels midi jump fra limb to limb,
Di birds midi play she and him
Chirping wildly here and dere
Dey fanned dem tails fu ketch di air.
Da mid merry month of May,
Da mi wa hat and summer day
Wen Ilda Almira Veronica rose
Gawn da bush, fu try fu push,
Fu times me hawd and praise de Lawd,
Di man whe she gat
Neva woth di lawd
Whe she put inna di Johnny cake
Fu mek he eat.
Sop Ilda Almira Veronica Rose
Put on she ole time tear up clothes.
And den she set on di ole straw hat
Fu cova up some big time plat
Whe she wear pan tap a she head
Like hair style mi just done dead.
Machete inna she hand
And bag crass she back,
Ilda Almira Veronica Rose
Da plantation gawn flap.
But she worried, worried,
No know whe she wa du
If di mango done gawn walk pan foot,
Or if di plantain, banana dem done di cook,
Or maybe di yam and cassava done de da shap,
Or di coco done de inna somebody pat.
So, Ilda Almira Veronica Rose,
She worried, worried fra head to toes.
Oh dis merry merry month of May!
Oh dis hat hat summer day!
And all would a mi bi all right

Except fu wan big majority fack.
Yu si, Ilda Almira Veronica rose
Mi gwen go reap whe she neva sows.
And no matta whe, mi dear, yu do
Wickedness wa always ketch right up wit yu.
So wen Ilda almira Veronica Rose
To di plantation mi draw close
She peep fu si da whe dide,
And, she worried bad fu she me hear
Dat proprietor, Mr. Ezeikel Hurryfoot,
Fast de ada kina way de to.
And dough she be wa experienced woman,
She still believed she just and right
And she know she'd hav fu fight
Fu protect she innocence
Whe lang gone one night.
But den suppose Eziekel bring police?
She close she mind fu get wa lee ease.
She worried to fu she mi hear
Tata Duende mi roaming right round dere.
And she mi hear he midi luk fu wife
And she wouldn't waa he fu de death a she life.
But, anyway, she staut to creep
And somewhere all she peep and peep.
Little did she, howeva, know
Ezeikel follow close below.
He angry fu no first time todey
Dey bin di thief am witout delay.
Sucka afta sucka hc bury da ground.
Sucka afta sucks come chap dem down.
Many a days Ezeikel bring hi sac,
Y go back home empty crass hi back.
So now at last he wa ketch wa thief
And wen he ketch a-thief wa shake like leaf.
Oh Ezeikel happy disya day
Fu at last y di happen fu wat he mi pray,
All inna hi mind he know whe he wa do:
He wa beat di thief, mash a, turn a inna fufu.
Ezeikel calm down wandring whe fu do:
Chap a, shoot a, or kick a inna hi –oops.
But den somting strange ketch Ezeikel eyes
Fu unda di hat de, di big plat dem he spy.
Ezeikel know dat now man hair inna style
But plat like dende he neva si fu wa wile.
So den he realize, da no man dis a tal.

Da wa woman di Thies am. Dis beyond recall.
And so di story change, hi face staut to smile.
Sweet tings through hi mind, hi bady wiggle a lee wile.
All Ezeikel prayers dem answered da di plantation todey;
So fu tank di good Lawd he kneel down and pray.
Oh happiness burst Ezeikel heart apart,
But he tink clearly, he no waa no false staut.
So he mek up hi face like he angry and mad
So dat wen he request di thief wa only glad
Fu giva whe he want fu good or fu bad.
Or, he wa tell she he wa tie ha up; teka da jail;
And de wa lak she up fueva, no giv a no bail.
So Ezeikel wit hi face mek up madda dan night
Touch di gial and giva such a fright.
She leap fra di ground she legs open wide
And Ezeikel midi right de: pacing astride.
Po Ilda Almira Veronica Rose,
She so frighten she tremble, she whole bady froze.
She no know whe fu se, can't talk, can't even lie.
No prayers she se even thou she gwen die.
And Ezeikel wit hi face mek up madda dan night,
Strat round and round di gial fra lef to di right
Wit gun inna wa hand and machete da y height.
She tremble and tremble wit fright afta fright.
Den slowly she smile. Ezeikel like wat he si.
And as she turn on di pose Ezeikel lick tongue wit glee
And hi eyes dem did crass and hi foot staut to tremble.
But den he catch himself-da no su fu do dis.
If she know how he weak, da she wa get everyting.
But she turn on di pose, he no know whe fu do.
He kneel down fu touch she hand but she play hawd fu get.
He figet she midi thief am. He wa figet lat mo yet.
So he decide fu offa ha wa bunch a banana.
She hurry agree fu she like wat could be.
So he sharpen hi machete, as nervous as he be,
But wen he turn round fu chap at di tree,
Wit all di evil dat could possible be,
Was Tata Duende instead a di tree.
Po Ezeikel he frighten. He tink he done dead.
Wit all di gial leg he cova up hi head.
And now Ilda Almira Veronica Rose
Mi confused, she soon figet all bout pose.
She no know whe happen why Eziekel di stamma.
She look all round and si noting di matta.
So she rub hi head and she quieten am down

And slowly he peep here dere all around.
Eziekel di wanda if di sun mi to hat.
Deya vision hi si da mus di heat do dat.
So slowly he get up. He feel kina shame.
Now, di gial wa talk and bring down hi name.
So he pick up hi machete and gat ready fu chap
And dis time we he si, Ezeikel know, da neva sun dud at.
He leggo hi machete and he run and he run,
And dey se he mi run till di sun come down.
So Ilda Almira Veronica Rose
Decide fu get up fra outa she pose;
Fu curiosity did get di betta a she
And she waa si da whe happen wit he.
So slowly she walk and circle di tree
But noting she si, between yu and me.
But den she hear like wa sound behind,
But maybe da only wa lee animal di climb.
She stop again fu she tink she hear,
So den she decide she betta move quickly fra dere.
But too late fu po Ilda Almira Veronica Rose
Fu Tata Duende mi like she si pose,
And di life gone bye she betta figet.
So po Ilda Almira Veronica Rose,
She slide to di ground fu wa quiet doze.
And Tata Duende call hi jungle friends
And away dey took ha to get ready fu di end.
And as yu know, Tata Duende da fra di magic land,
So di jungle gat ready wit wa magic band.
And so y mi de fu all dem folks fu si
Di loveliest wedding dat wa eva be.

From *The Son of Kinnich* (Dangriga: Jaribu Books, 1995), 113-119

Excerpt from <u>*The House of Snakes*</u>

By Dr. Colville Young

[. . .] "You see," said Tanny, "I did overhear Paisano talking 'bout how he would paddle a dorey-load of fruit and vegetable to Belize and live wid one o' e' cousin dem. I make sure he really lef' wid' e oversize dorey loaded down wit de fruit an' vegetable.

"Den ah take de bigges' crocus beg ah could find an' ah hot-foot it to Paisano farm. Ah end up under the most bigges' mengo tree on de farm. Ah t'row me scabbard wid de machete in it to one side so it would'n get in me way, den ah start to climb, headun' fo' de limb loaded wid de most mengo dem. Ah get dere an' shake an' shake. Biggi-dif boof! Biggi-dif boof! Pure mengo fallin', de bigges', ripes', sweetes' of judge-wig[1]. Den ah do de same wid four, five mo' limb an' after dat decide to come down an' begin fullin' up de crocus beg.

"But as ah get to de foot o' de tree, wha you t'ink happen? A fin' de begges wowler[2] you could even begin to dream 'bout waitin' an' watchin', watchin' and' waitin ' fo me.

"Sometin 'bout dis snake, an' de way it watch me, was strange. It was as if de creeta intelligent somehow, as if it readin' me mind. Plus, as ah mention a' ready, it was really huge, at leas' twenty feet; dough ah had very little inclination to measure de brute. Now, some pipple t'ink a wowler is a pisonous snake but I know a wowler is not a pisonous snake-jus' a biter, jus' a crusher an' a squeezer an' a biter an' a eater. Dat's all.

"So ah tu'n roun' to get me meachete where ah did t'row it on de groun' in de scabbard befo' climbin' de mengo tree.

"An' what de hell you t'ink ah find? Two yellow-jaw tommy goff,[3] which is de deadlies' of pisonous snakes in Belize, dere waitin' fo me. Ah no frighten yet, but ah beginnin' to sweat an' blow hard. Ah look 'roun ' quick quick quick an' locate a stick. Ah jus' about to ben' down an' pick it up when, as dere's a god above, de stick tu'n into a t'ird tommy-gaff.

"Well you could imagine is now ah frighten fo' 'fraid! One minute ah' reachin' fo' a black stick on de groun' an' de nex' minute de stick change to a red snake wid yellow triangle dem runnin' down di side an' underneat' o' de jaw yellow like wid all tommy goff.

"Now I, Atelstan Williams, is a brave man, willing to take on de devil an' all 'is angels dem. But dis was too much. Ah tu'n to run; ah say to meself, foot wha you make for! But as ah jus' about to run, de snakes bar de way, raisin' deir head an' shoulder off of de groun' wid dere tongue goin' in an' out, in an' out. Dey don't attack, jus' res' dere watchin' me wid eye like is coloured bead shinin' in de sun. An' ah havin' dis feelin', like ice water runnin' down me back, dis feelin' dat dese snakes have intelligence, dat somehow dey lookin' straight into me mind de way a man or woman would look into a room. Dat is one feelin' ah never ever want to experience again! You hear me, compe? Never, ever, never ever again!

"Well, now, dark comin' an' ah decide to go into de farmhouse an' dey allow me to pass easy, buy dey following' an dey watchin' every move a make. Ah find a hurricane lamp in de kitchen an' a box o' match nearby. Ah light de lamp an' heng it from a crossbeam. All dis time ah so frighten dat ah fraid fo me own shadow-an' every move ah move the de feeble light form dat hurricane – lamp cast a different shadow, on de floor, on de wall, on de ileskin dat cover de table.

"Dis time, ah beginning' to feel hungry but ah bite it in, bite it in, till it start to get late an' soon like how ah never eat since mornin', me belly start to wonder if me t'roat cut or what. So ah look roun' to see if Paisano have any provisions in de house. Ah fin de usual: coffee an' tea an' sugar an' some tins of condense milk, an' a sack o' flour an bittles like dat.

"So ah take me courage wid a good grip an' begin to prepare a meal. All dis time, snakes watchin' me. Dey watch me but dey don't say not'n, dey don't do not'n.

"So ah pour kerosene in Paisano etna, light it, put the frying pan on de fire wid coconut ile coverin' de bottom. Den a knead up some flour an' water an' lard an' salt an' make fry jacks. Den a put on water to bile in de kettle an' make meself some coffee in a enamel cup which ah find on de kitchen dresser. Ah find a piece o' cheese an' strange enough, in spite of de way de snakes terrorize me, a really enjoy dat meal. I suppose when man hungry an' nature call, dat's it!

"Friends, ah coulda never explain de res' o' dat terrible night. Leavin' de farm was out o' de question. Ah need sleep de way a newborn infant need de titty. But how de hell fo sleep wid dem devil snake dere watchin' an waiting, waitin' an' watching! Ah lay down on Paisano bed an' count de hours, minute by minute, an' every minute was sixty seconds of mental agony an fear. Ah look at de floor roun' de bed every now an' again, an' every time is snakes ah make out in de lamp-light.

"[. . .] But de whole whole night ah don't once get up, not even for a pee, till de sun shinin' into de room wake me up. Fos t'ing ah do is tenk Massa dat life spare. Nex' t'ing ah do is look to see if de snakes gone. Gone where! Dey right dere watchin' an' waitin'.

"Well, ah get up an' dey allow me. Ah wash out me mout' an' clean up an' work up some bittles to eat, den walk cross to Paisano house of lords 'bout twenty-five feet from de house an do the usual, den try again to edge me way off de farm. But de moment ah try dat, de snakes bar de way. Den suddenly de t'ought enter me head dat sinc as was goin' to be pen up in dat farm like dat, ah might as well make meself useful, if you see wha ah mean.

"So ah get me meachete –dis time dey 'low me to do dis. But by now dey have me so frighten ah woulda as soon try fo chop de breeze as try to chop one o' dem snakes. Ah tek de machete an' begin to clean out de bush on de farm: trimmin' de trees, cutting de grass wherever it too high. An' ah do dis every day for a week till dat farm was as neat an' tidy as de garden at Government House. An' all dis time de snakes watchin' an' waitin.' First t'ing in de mornin' is snake, last t'ing at night is snake. Snake watchin' you eat, snake followin' you to de damn latrine an' every dream you dream when you sleep is pack wid snake, not'n but snake!

"Well, me compe, to cot a long story short, after one week of dat, along come Paisano himself. Ah look at him an can't mek up me mind whedder ah glad to see 'im or sorry. Ah glad because ah know only he coulda ever release me from de burden o' dem snakes, since he control dem, you understan'! Which in, at de same time ah don't know wha he goin' to do to me to punish me fo trespassin' on his property.

"So ah watch him get out of his dorey an' tie it up by de benk-side. Den 'e lif' out a pataki from de dorey-a pataki is wha' country pipple like him use in place of a valise. Ah go to meet him by de river wid you-know-who troopin' along behind me! Ah decide to talk fos an' ah say to him like dis:

'Paisano my neighbour! How t'ings goin', man? How was de trip to Belize?'

'Wat you doin' on me lan'? Paisano growl at me like a bad bulldog.

'Jus bein' a good neighbour, as I say,' I reply. 'Ah was noticin' how de bush grow too t'ick an' de grass too high on your farm. So ah jus' decide to gie you a little help because of bein' a good neighbour.

'An because eof de snakes, eh!' And dat little waika-man grin a evil grin wid 'is yellow teet.

'You make frien' wid de snakes, eh? De wowler, he bad 'nough. But de yellow-jaw! De yellow-jaw! Eh? Eh?'

'At dat, ah tu'n to pick up me crocus beg an' to lef de place in peace. But as ah reach down to get it, Paisano say, "Wha you doin' wid dat bag, now?' I say to him, 'Dis bag belongs to me. I bring it 'ere an' ah takin' it away. See, Paisano, it empty empty.'

'Put it down; lef it where it lay,' Paisano say, an' p'int his double-barrel shotgun straight at me heart. When ah see dat, an' see de snakes still ready an' waitin' for anytin' to start, ah decide to lap me tail an' head fo' home.

'An' you lucky you get away wid de clothes on you teefing backside.' Paisano shout at me as ah leave, an' 'e laugh an' laugh. An' so ah walkin' away down de picado road away from 'e farm, so de laughter follering me."

From *Pataki Full* by Colville Young (Belize: Cubola Productions, 1991), 16-23

Excerpt from Misiyoun

By Jessie Nuñez Castillo

[. . .] In Younton no one was rich, but the people were friendly and caring. They believed that strangers should always be given good hospitality. They often talked about some messenger of God, Misiyoun. Their stories were that he could come at any time, shabby, tired and hungry. Those who turned him away without food or drink always suffered misfortune. So any stranger was offered food and drink. Some people always cooked a little extra in case some hungry traveler happened to stop by. If the food was exact, the parents, usually the mother, shared a little of hers with the stranger. It did not matter if they knew the person or not. Chana had learned this from her grandmother, and shared cheerfully if she needed to. When things looked good, she cooked extra plantain and fish. Whoever stopped in at mealtime was welcome to what she had. One afternoon, Chana had found very little to cook. She had cooked barely enough plantain for her *hudutu* and a baby shark in the *fálumoun*. She was dishing out her children's food when a white man came to the door. When he said good afternoon, Chana smiled in response. He extended his hands to shake hers as he sadi, "I'm Larry, and how are you?." Chana looked at him and responded in garifuna. *"Laari! Ka ari?"* She did not understand what the man was saying, but she could not let him go by without something to eat. She smiled back and motioned for him to sit on a nearby stool. She quickly turned to get a plate so she could give him something to eat. Chana took a little from each of the children's plate and a little from hers to make the stranger a small one. She set the plate on the small table in her living room and motioned to the stranger, telling him in garifuna, *"Beiga wama."* (Eat with us). Tired and hungry from his walk in the warm tropical sun, the stranger gratefully accepted. "thank you," he said, as he picked up the spoon to taste the *fálumoun*. "Mmm, this is good." He ate a piece of the plantain and drank another spoonful of *fálumoun*. "Mmm, natural soup!" Chana was listening. She quickly stepped up to the table, picked up the plate of food and said; *"Baturali? Mayabibadibu aturei nufalumoun. Subuditi lidere nafagun bun! Dürüguarügü numuti heigin fugiabu nisanigu bun. Beiba nubiengien!"* (You'll throw it away? You can't come here and throw away my *fálumoun*. You don't know how hard I work to get this food! And I had to shorten my children's meal to give you some. Get out of my house."). Chana said all this in one breath, angry at what she thought the stranger had said. The poor stranger, confused by her reaction, walked out and went his way, tired, hungry and thirsty. The taste of the food lingered in his mouth for a while but he was afraid to go back or stop at another house in the village. Chana, however, would not mention the incident for a very long time. She was worried for a while that it was Misiyoun and that she would suffer even more misfortune. But, how was she to tell?

From *Memories, Dreams and Nightmares*, Vol. 2 (Cubola Books: Belize, 2005), pp.28-29

GRANNY'S STORIES
(NO. 1) HAG
(OLE HEG)

By J. S. Martínez

This tale that I shall now relate,
   Is one from granny's store;
And if it's pleasant to your taste,
   I'll likely give you some more;
But phrases queer of Granny's choice
   Although fine colours lend,
   Might prove a bit too puzzling
     For you to comprehend.

   "You picny now of disyer time,
    "You hab it good and fine;
"You run about and play da night,
    "Sometime till eight an nine;
   "Wen I me leel an stan like you,
    "No night could see me out:
    "Espece'ly wen I hear dem talk,
     "Dat 'Ole Heg' is about!"

And then she tells of Betsy Jane,
   A wrinkled withered dame;
How she had shed her human skin,
   And then a hag became—
With birdlike wings herself equipped
   At night to neighbours flew,
And while they slept, this hag with zest
   Their precious life blood drew.

But once when she was at her pranks
   Unknowing of a thief;
An artful lad her steps had dodged,
   And caused her anxious grief:
He took her skin, her human skin!
   And corned and peppered same
   So in a plight that hag was placed,
    When form her hunt she came.

For as the mortar she approached,
   In which her skin was lain;
She started to resume her from,

But lo! She groaned in pain:
For there before her eyes she saw
 Her brushed and battered cloak,
And knew that 'twas at her expense
 Someone had played a joke.

So in great anger she began
 To wash her peppered skin;
And when at last the job was done,
 She got herself within;
And so she cursed the human race,
 As only hags could do,
And swore to have her wrongs revenged,
 Before her term was through.

But once again when from her hunt,
 A grievance new she found—
Inside her hut, some Wangla Seeds
 Were scattered on the ground:
Now through the merit of some charm
 These little seeds possess,
Their presence hinders hags to gain
 Reentrance to their dress.

She then must pick them one by one,
 A long and irksome task;
The dawn was now commencing fast,
 To pierce night's gloomy mask.
The chagrined hag kept toiling on,
 But trembled fo'r the sun
Had peered into her shabby hut,
 Before her task was done.

Her task completed, Wretched Hag!
 Disheartened quite was she—
Her lofty pride could not endure
 Such gross indignity;
And so in shame and anguish sore,
 She threw aside her crown;
 So endeth then the reigning
 Of that last hag of our town.

Still, there are other hags about,
 Not skilled enough to fly,
 But yet are human menaces;'

    Their strings do testify;
Would that some method could be found
   To rid the town of these.
Then "Good Character" would be let
   To live in peace and ease.

From *Characters and Caricatures in Belizean Folklore* (Belize UNESCO Commission: Belize, 1991), pp.51-52

The Death of Anancy

Once upon a time Anancy, weary of home, journeyed far into the country on and on, until at last everywhere was new to him. It seemed to Anancy that the country he was now in was far more beautiful than any place he had ever seen, the grass greener and the cattle finer.

Approaching a pasture in which were hundreds of sheep, Anancy said to a man standing near, "An who dem fat sheep belong to,sar?"

"Death" was the reply.

"Deat?" An' who am him?" queried Anancy, but the stranger had moved by.

"An' demy ere cows, who dem belong to?" he asked the next passerby.

"Death" came the whisper in a frightened voice.

A young, happy child came dancing along the road.

"Pickney, who dem goat fo?" asked Anancy, stopping her as she was about to pass.

Laughing gaily, she called out, "To Death, of course," and ran on.

An old woman came tottering by, and Anancy went to her, "Who dem fields belong to, ole missis?"

"Death," came the answer in a voice that shook with fear.

"Deat'," said Anancy. "Strange me nebber hear oh Bredda Deat, an him have de best of everything in de world."

"True, true," quavered the old woman, "the very best, the very best in all the world."

"Me would like meet him fer true."

"Hush! Hush!" replied the woman, "You no want meet him, fer what you do, no good fer yer cry an bawl, he tek yer and dat's de end of yer; so turn and go back befo he catches sight oh yer."

"But why? A genman, what has got so much, ain't he kind an' good?"

"Kind, yes, but to very few, an dcruel, oh! Cruel to as many. Tears does follow his footsteps and hearts done break wherever he go."

"An' all dis land an all dem fat fat cattle belong to him.?"

"All."

"An' nobody ever tief dem?'

"Steal from Death? No one can do dat," said the woman, sadly, moving away.

"La me, massa, "laughed Anancy, "but me tink Anancy can tief from anybody, so ge get de chance."

Anancy walked on and came to a big iron gate, above which was written "DEATH."

"So," said Anancy, "dis am where he libs. La, jest look at de cows, an pigs an' an' fowls inside dar. Me must get in dar, sure. Open gate; open me good gate, do."

But although the gate creaked, it did not open, and after thinking a moment, Anancy caught a young ting pig that was wandering about outside, killed it and greased the hinges of the gate with some of the fat. Immediately the gate flew open, and Anancy fairly rushed through.

Running up a broad avenue, he suddenly came upon a being whose appearance was so awe-inspiring that even Anancy staggered back, but quickly recovering himself, he removed his hat and made a sweeping bow.

"Marnin, sah, Bredda Deat," but there was no reply. "Me would like fer see yer house. Yer no mind?"

Still no reply; so Anancy proceeded to the house and, as he passed through put in his capacious pockets whatever he fancied.

Happening to glance up, he saw Death regarding him gravely.

"You no mind me teke dis few little things, jest fer remember yer by?" Receiving no reply, Anancy went on to the garden.

"Ye tink me would like dat big black horse, but you no like ter say so? Nebber mind, me will tek it. And dem fowl, ye tink me better hab a few? Well, jest oblige," and tying a great number of fowls together, Anancy flung them on the horse and mounted himself.

Turning to death, he said, "Tanks, Bredda Deat,' you is genman fer true, eben if you no can talk, an me will cum again, nebber fear, and me will bring all me chillen wid me, so dey get presents too."

Anancy now urged the horse on, but he went slowly and Death followed silently and sternly.

They had now come to the gate, and Anancy called, "Open gate!"

"Open not!" thundered Death in a voice that made Anancy sick with fright.

"Open, do open, me good gate," begged Anancy, "see how me ease your pain with da fat of a young pig? You couldn't be so ungrateful like."

The gate opened slowly and but a little bit, but Anancy galloped through just before the gate again swung to.

He laughed loudly and turned to throw some defiant remark at Death on the other side of the gate, but to his horror Death sat behind him on the horse and held him tight.

He met a man on the road, and pulling up the horse, Anancy called out to him:—"Do me, Massa; cum tek dis genman off a me back."

The man started to obey, but when he came nearer and saw who sat behind, he drew back hurriedly and ran away.

Riding on, he met another and beseeched him tearfully to come and take away his hateful companion, but this man also refused.

He came at last to a woman, and thinking to find her more tender-hearted, pulled up the horse and and begged her to take Death from off his back.

"Dat can't be done," she replied mournfully. "Nobody can take Death from another, howsoever much they may wish fer to do so. When Death comes fer yer, it's you he will hab, and cry as you may, groan as you will, go you muss."

Some laughed heartlessly at his plight; others took no notice. They had sen Death come to their fellows so often.

On and on, faster and faster, until, as they drew near Anancy's home, he felt Death's grip on him relax, and when he pulled up at his own door, he made one mighty effort and threw Death from him.

Dismounting, he grappled with his foe and at last vanquished him. Death lay at his feet. Thinking to make an end of him, Anancy rushed indoors for his machete, but when he returned Death had disappeared.

The next morning Anancy awakened early, and going outside his hut, saw a fine kyalaloo growing beside his doorstep. Calling his wife, he bade her cut the kyalaloo and make him some soup.

"Me no touch dat Kyalaloo," said his wife. "Don't you see dat it grow up overnight on de zack same spot you trew down Bredda Deat?"

"Bring you de carving knife?" answered his wife, pretending not to hear. Anancy insisted, but his wife flatly refused, and at last, getting in a rage, he cut the kyalaloo himself, and bolied a fine pot of soup, which he immediately ate.

Soon after he felt as if he had eaten fire-he was scorching to death. "Hi, dar," he called to his wife, "bring me some water; me inside am on fire."

"Water! Water!" screamed Anancy.

"Kerosene ile?" screamed his wife.

"Water-do, me love, fetch me some water."

"Red peeper? Is dat what you want?"

And Anancy, shrieking and groaning, slowly burnt up.

And his wife, returning to the hut to prepare her own dinner, ejaculated, "Serve him well, an' right! He dat greedy!"

And this was the end of Anancy, who, in spite of his great cunning, could not elude Death when Death came for him.

From *Characters and Caricatures in Belizean Folklore*, (Belize UNESCO Commission, Belize, 1991), pp. 11-13

Chaper 5

Romantic Love

Miriam

By Ishmael Flores

Just that branching of the road
Just that fork on the trail
Only that detour on the way;
The easiest way that I chose to travel on
Has made all the difference in my life.

Two persons; a fork on the trail; a chasm in between
Just a difference in the path we chose
And the whisper of a living memory
A maze of faces in the dark
A kaleidoscope of colors in my mind.

Miriam, do you remember when I first saw you?
The way our eyes met the way you lowered your head
First impressions are not always right
But mine of you was perfect from the start
Much madness it was, Oh Spanish girl.

Yet our souls stretched out their hands and met
Across the vast depth of space and time
They understood each other without a spoken word
Yet our destinations, two worlds apart
Are traveling on their own well-trodden paths.

Just that passage in time, in the past
Just a meeting of two souls without our consent
Yet never a spoken word to us, our mortal selves
And always that treacherous fork on the road
That has made all the difference in my life.

From *Belizean Poets, Part 3* (Government Printers: Belize, circa 1972), p. 23

The Fisherman's Wife and the Storm

By Dr. Henry Anderson

I touch my toes to the tormented sands
And waves wash with wails of wind.
I look; I search but I cannot see.
My love labours far out at sea,
My love labours far away from me.

Clouds build bursting blue skies
And rains torment in torrents
The very sands on which I stand.
My love, are you safe at sea?
My love, have you been taken from me?

No seagulls grace the tempest skies;
Thunder darkens their distant cries.
Lightening! No white feathered breast.
My love, will you return to me
Or are you among coral deep at sea?

Storms sail terrors in my mind,
Waves wreck! Wring me crushed,
Yet I have loved upon this shore
Just you sea, my love and me.
But mostly this tormented life,
Lot to the fisherman's wife.
Oh God I pray for his safety at sea,
I embrace his hardship should he sail home to me.

At times I pray that this would end,
Some other life this life would lend;
But strong is the call of the savage sea
And each day he goes away from me.
It's life, to his mistress, it is to be.

Battles have raged, ships have sunk,
Riches have been lost: gold laden trunks,
Men have drowned, women, children too;
Yet men return to the sea
Subjects of nature's captivity.

I am beached with worries, forlorn,
Waiting hopeful amidst the storms,

Not worried if the nets have made a catch
But hopefully only that he returns to me,
My fisherman far out at sea.

I touch my toes to the tormented sands
And waves wash with wails of wind.
I look, I search but I cannot see.
My love labours far out at sea,
My love labours far away from me.

From *The Son of Kinnich* (Jaribu Books: Dangriga, Belize, 1995), pp. 25-26

For the First Time

By Sur Jim Arnold, B.A (Bachelor of Antics)

For the first time
    I never felt this way before
       For the first time
  I had to let my feelings show
I couldn't hide but I had to let her know
  This must be love for sure
     For the first time.

  I knew from my heart
  As I looked in her eyes
  The tenderness of love
  Was what I recognize
  I didn't see no color
For that doesn't matter
I fell in love I tell you
With this pretty Spanish girl.

She couldn't speak good English
 And I cannot speak good Spanish
But no further explanation about communication
For our only destination—we understand our love
     For the first time.

Now inquiring minds want to know
  What's the difference in our age
Well, I would like to write a book
  Explaining of every page
But we can't please everyone
And only few will understand.

Love is so innocent
   And so true
Love turns old into new
Love whats to be has got to be
Love don't see age in you and me
But welcome sincerity
For the first time.

From *Kriol and English Poems* (Peni Printers: Belize, 1998), p. 15

Idyllic Love

By Rudolph Smith

One March my love and I did stroll,
Where multi-coloured flowers grew.
From one such bush I stole
And gave my love a daisy wet with dew.
With tender eyes she kissed my lips
And whispering softly said: "On land
Or sea no gift shall ever eclipse
This lovely daisy now in my hand."

Over all June's warmth had swept one morn,
Distilling in the air its sweet perfume;
I picked from off a prickly thorn
And gave my love a rose in bloom.
With tender sighs she kissed my eyes
And whispering softly said: "Heart of bliss,
Nothing on earth or in the skies
Will be so deeply prized as this."

To fierce September the months did yield.
One flower alone withstood its deadly glare;
It gambolled proudly in a field.
I gave my love this orchid rare;
With tender sighs she kissed my mouth,
And whispering softly said: "I love you,
And with this orchid now I pledge my troth
Not even death will make me be untrue."

But when gaunt December shed its light,
Across the narrowed border of the year,
As if twas readying for a wider flight;
I gave my love a lily for her bier.
"O Love," I whispered; and her dear eyes
Smiled through the unquickened clay.
"Love should be something which never dies
For God is love, and he over all holds sway."

From *Belizean Poets, Part 3* (Government printers: Belize, circa 1972), p. 70

Excerpt from **Y el metro me lleva a casa**

By Zoila Ellis, translated by Omar Fuentes

[. . .] Después de pagar, se marchó. Cuando caminaba a casa, no podía dejar de comprender la impecabilidad de los alrededores del lugar en el que trabajaba con la calle en que vivía. A lo largo de toda esta calle se encontraban desparramadas latas de cerveza aplastadas y otras porquerías. Por todas partes se oían ruidos, gritos y carcajadas.

Los hombres que jugaban a las apuestas en la esquina la silbaban al pasar: " Nena, ¿te enrolla un poco de *maría*?" Russell le aconsejó que no les hiciera caso y eso hacía, pero aun así, odiaba aquello. Caminando apresuradamente llegó hasta el portal, subió a la entrada e introdujo la llave en la cerradura.

"El momento en que sientas miedo de tu vecindario, es el momento de mudarse," decía un anuncio de una inmobiliaria. Es posible que vendiera esta casa y comprara otra en un vecindario mejor. Tal vez. Porque mudarse era una lata.

Olió el pollo que se freía en la cocina. Era agradable que Russell cocinara. Siempre hacía cosas encantadoras como ésa.

—Russell Lawrence, buenas noches, señor.

—Señorita Jones. ¿Cuándo llegó? Deme un beso, ¿no? ¿Cómo está la chica más hermosa del mundo? –avanzó para abrazarla. Ella le rechazó juguetonamente.

—Suéltame, chico. Apesto. Tengo mucho calor.

El la miró lasciva.

—¡Ya! Lo que quieres es una cerveza o . . . —ella fingió no entender.

—No, una ducha antes de cualquier cosa . . .

—Está bien, caramelito.

Cantaba en voz baja para sí misma bajo la ducha. Russell era realmente un encanto. Después de todo, quizá debería considerar casarse con él. Y luego, claro, ¿ y si fuera lo único que estuviera buscando? Casarse para, entonces, atarla. Poco tiempo después de la boda no volvería a verla nunca más. Igual que Charles. No, era mejor mantenerse soltera. Además, tenía asuntos importantes que resolver. Tal vez después. Ahora, estaba a gusto tal y como estaba.

Escuchó a lo lejos el insistente sonar del teléfono. Su cuerpo estaba caliente debajo y feliz mientras el agua ardiendo le masajeaba los hombros cansados.

"Probablemente sea Joanna," pensó distraída, inhalando profundamente la suave esencia de la loción de baño que le encantaba. Russell irrumpió sacándola bruscamente de su somnoliento estado.

—¡Es para ti, cariño, de Belice!

—¡Ya voy!—respondió, poniéndose a toda prisa el albornoz mientras cogía el auricular que estaba colocado convenientemente al lado de la ducha.

—¿Hola? Habla Carla.

—Hola, ¿mamá? Soy yo, Junie—Escuchó que él tomaba un profundo respiro y luego proseguía apresuradamente—Te llamo para decirte que me casé con Sarita esta mañana.

El esperó callado. Ella no podía hablar. El auricular se cayó al suelo.

—¿Mamá? ¿Mamá? ¿Sigues allí? ¿Hola? ¿Hola?

Carla miró fijamente el auricular del teléfono, los sonidos que salían de ahí parecían afiladas agujas de hielo que golpeaban su cuerpo enfriándolo gradualmente. Observando el auricular rosado que pendía de un lado a otro, rezaba para que la pena no le rompiera el corazón.

From *De Héroes, Iguanas y Pasiones*, Trans. By Omar Fuentes (Ediciones Zanzíbar: Madrid, 2003), pp. 140-142

Excerpt from *A conscience for Christmas*

By Evan X Hyde

[. . .] And as they walked towards the door, Joanna's drunken bitchy voice screamed in his ears. "And where do you two think you're going, Mr. Caldo?" He slapped Joanna. The band had stopped playing as he walked out with the girl in the yellow maxi. What was the matter with him? He wasn't drunk. He was just tired of being smooth with fools.

He asked her how old she was and she said eighteen and what was her name and she said Tricia and he remembered something but exactly what it was escaped him.

"Where are we going?" she asked.

"Home."

"Did you ask me?"

"No," he said. "I love you."

She held his arm and looked up at him. Her eyes were wet. "Do you mean it, Caldo? Please say you mean it, Caldo. I love you from a long time. I see you going to work, sometimes at night I see you passing with girls. I want to be with you, Caldo, anywhere you go, please." She was crying softly on his chest.

He felt a complete fool. He wanted to tell her to stop crying on his shirt or she would mess it up. But Caldo knew this was one girl he could never do that to. She was a child at heart, and Christmas, he mused to himself, it was for children. Run away, Caldo, he said to himself, run away from her, or she will be the end of you. Run away now, Caldo, run away from the softness of your heart.

He remembered her now. She was a primary school teacher. He'd seen her in uniform before, but never in a soft yellow maxi. No, Caldo, take her home with you. She will be so easy. When you are finished, wash your hands, wipe your mouth, and move on, move on.

He kissed her quickly to gain time. She wanted to linger but he would not.

"Let's go," he held her hand. "What are you doing hanging around with Joanna?

Don't you know what she is?" His voice was gruff.

"I wanted to go to the party. I knew you would be there. My grandmother didn't want to send me. Are you vex?"

"Who's your grandmother?"

"Miss Gertrude, don't —?"

He couldn't hear any more. Damn, there was a jinx on him. This was obeah business. Miss Gertrude, the little old woman who melted his heart on Christmas Eve. And now it was Christmas and her granddaughter was eating out what was left of his heart. Him, Caldo, Caldo the executioner, Lone Ranger Caldo, smooth Caldo, he was caught, trapped.

Damn, come on, girl, let's go home by Miss Gertrude. We'll drink the berry wine, the three of us, we'll talk, laugh and be merry. When the cock crows, we'll go to church, the three of us, what a way, and then we'll walk the streets and watch the children playing, the drunks and serenaders, me and you and Miss Granny. We'll visit my sister and your people. Damn, I'll take you and Miss Gertrude to my home. Christmas comes but once a year. He looked down at her. She was just a baby girl, and Christmas was for children.

From *Snapshots of Belize*, Ed. Michael Phillips (Cubola Productions: Belize, 1995) pp.46-48

Excerpt from **La Llorona**

Por David Ruiz Puga

—¡María Alejandra! ¡María Alejandra!

Don Salvador se encontraba sentado en la mesa junto a doña Paulina, su mujer, quien estaba absorta en su bordado. Sostenía él, entre sus manos una breve carta que había recibido esa mañana. La había leído varias veces y por fin, se sentó para discutir el asunto con su esposa. Entonces, decidieron tomar en cuenta a María Alejandra de diecisiete años, la mayor de sus hijas, quien era indiscutiblemente la persona con más derecho a oír el contenido de aquella carta.

María Alejandra apareció apresuradamente a la puerta secándose las manos en el delantal rojo que llevaba enlazada en la cintura. Era una señorita muy hermosa, de cuerpo bien formado y facciones muy finas. Tenía piel clara, pelo largo, lacio, y negro como la noche; la belleza de sus largas pestañas se complementaba con una nariz larga y respingada y una sonrisa dulce y tierna.

—Mande papá—dijo sumisamente.

—Oye nada más—respondió don Salvador, acercándose al papel—"Muy respetable Señor Salvador Ibarra Montenegro. . . . " Don Salvador se detuvo, volteó la cara hacia un lado y tosió. Y continuó leyendo en voz alta—"Me dirijo a usted con todo respeto añorando que usted y su distinguida familia estén gozando de las bendiciones de nuestro Creador. . . ."

Don Salvador se detuvo por segunda vez y, echándole una mirada a doña Paulina, quien escuchaba atentamente con bordado en le regazo, dijo:

—¡Muy buen saludo de este muchacho!

Fue entonces cuando María Alejandra, que había permanecido de pie, levantó el rostro y, tratando de ocultar su emoción, se le acercó tímidamente a su padre.

—Muchacha—dijo don Salvador—, veo que te emocionas. ¿Acaso estás enterada de eso?

—¡No, papá!—mintió María Alejandra bajando el rostro mientras doña Paulina la miraba inquietamente.

—"El propósito de la presente es para solicitarle a usted, permiso para visitar formalmente y cortejar a su dulce hija, María Alejandra. . . ."

Don Salvador se detuvo y miró a su hija quien trataba de esconder una sonrisa que se le escapaba de entre los labios.

—María Alejandra, ¿conoces tú a Macario de Jesús?

Doña Paulina, deduciendo que todo eso se ponía un poco tenso, interrumpió.

—Ha bailado una o dos veces con ella en el Salón Victoria; parece ser muy caballeroso.

—Ah, ¡entonces lo conoces!—exclamó don Salvador. Y diciendo esto, siguió leyendo.

—"Sepa usted, Señor Ibarra, que mis intenciones para con su hija son nobles. Le pido pues, que me otorgue usted una oportunidad para que su hija y yo nos tratemos y nos unamos eventualmente, si Dios lo permite, por medio del sagrado vínculo del matrimonio."

Don Salvador, sin terminar de leer la carta, la dobló y la puso en su sobre. Luego, se la metió en el bolsillo de la camisa.

—Hija—dijo—, puedes irte. Voy a pensarlo bien.

—Papá—suplicó María Alejandra—, por favor. . . .

—María Alejandra—repitió el padre alzando la voz —, dije que puedes retirarte.

—Sí papá—contestó la joven dándose la vuelta para salir de la sala.

Don Salvador se levantó y se dirigió hacia el estante que estaba en una esquina. Bajó una bolsa y sacó su pipa negra y una bolsita que contenía tabaco. Doña Paulina seguía todos los movimientos de su esposa esperando que diera veredicto.

—Paulina—comenzó don Salvador—, espero que cuides bien de María Alejandra cada vez que salen.

—¿Qué quieres decir, Salvador?—inquirió doña Paulina asentando sobre la mesa a la par de ella la funda que bordaba.

—María Alejandra ya es toda una señorita-contestó don Salvador—, y tenemos que tener mucho cuidado con estos pretendientes que andan como buitres para ver a quien devoran.

—Ella también es mi hija, Salvador—dijo la señora—. Ella no baila con cualquier vago y, cuando reparten la limonada y las galletas, me aseguro que esté a mi lado.

—¿Y de qué familia viene este tal Macario de Jesús?—preguntó don Salvador mientras llenaba su pipa de tabaco.

—¡Ah!—contestó doña Paulina —. Es hijo de don Pedro y de doña Margarita. Viven a la entrada del pueblo.

—Sí, conozco a don Pedro. ¿Y qué hace el muchacho?

—Ayuda a don Gabriel en la carpintería.

Don Salvador se había sentado. Miraba a su señora mientras fumaba su pipa y, después de unos instantes de silencio, dijo:

—Hablaré con el muchacho esta noche.

—¿Esta noche?—preguntó sorprendida doña Paulina.

—¡Claro! Dice que pasará esta noche por acá.

—¿Y qué vas a decirle?

—Pues . . . pues . . . —murmuró don Salvador pensativamente—, creo que le daré una oportunidad.

Ya dicha la última palabra, don Salvador se levantó y se dirigió hacia el patio. Doña Paulina dio un profundo suspiro de alivio y continuó bordando.

[. . .]

María Alejandra no se había quedado con las ganas de conocer la decisión de su padre al respecto. Se había metido al cuarto adyacente a la sala mientras sus padres hablaban y se había puesto a husmear. Y no renegó para cuando su madre la mandó a llevarle maíz a la tía Romelia que vivía contiguo a la iglesia. María Alejandra sentía que rebosaba de alegría, y quien mejor que la tía Mela, su confesora, para compartir su gran emoción.

Y ya en la cocina de la tía, la sobrina conversaba muy entusiasmada con ella.

—María Alejandra, no trates de esconderme nada que yo he sido como tu mejor amiga-continuó la tía Mela acercándose a la sobrina.

—¡Cómo es uste', tía!—exclamó María Alejandra indignada por lo que había dicho la tía—Lo que pasa es que en noches de luna cuando salgo a pasear con Carmelita y sus hermanas, Macario nos encuentra por la plaza.

—¡Virgen Santísima!—exclamó la tía—, no me hagas pensar cosas que no debo.

—Ay no, tía. Yo nunca me atreviera a hacer cosas malas como tomarse de las manos o besarse.

—Claro que no hija. Esas caricias antes del matrimonio son malas. Cuidado hija, que el besotearse lleva a otras cosas que no me atrevo a mencionar.

—Sí, tía—dijo María Alejandra con mucho respeto; y abriendo los ojos apasionadamente, dijo:

—Yo sólo me conformo con mirarle a los ojos. Siento que hasta la cabeza me da vueltas.

Y tomándole las manos a su tía, preguntó:

—Tía Mela, ¿uste' cree que estoy enamorada?

—Pues, mirando como te dan vuelta los ojos, yo diría que sí—contestó la tía Romelia sonriéndose.

From *Old Benque* (Cubola Productions: Benque Viejo del Carmen, 1990), pp. 72-77

Volverás

Por Nadia Hamze

Vas . . . hasta la otra parte
del mundo . . .
Tratas de ahogarte en otros brazos.
Buscas el más tierno amor
en tu camino . . .
Borras mi nombre de tus labios.
Matas cada sentimiento
que has tenido por mí.
Matas las ansias de nuestro amor.
Yo sé que volverás
con más amor y más celos
Porque dentro de ti
Llevas solamente mi amor.
Tú vas a buscar las perlas
de mis ojos en cada cara.
Y vas a buscar el olor
De mi cabello en cada belleza.
Y cuando te canses
De tu aberración,
Regresarás a mi buen amor
Porque tus sueños no viven
Sin mis sueños..
Y tu alma no puede morir
Lejos de mi alma.

From *Destiny: A Collection of Poems*, by Nadia Hamze

Chaper 6

Era of Independence and Protest

Birth of a Nation

By Milton Arana

This is a rugged land, a wild land, nature's country
And amply blessed and filled her with great bounty.
Nature resents the taming hand of man
And labours ever to frustrate his plan.
Cast back, dear friend, your eyes to long ago
And see that ancient Maya toiling slow:
See how he labours, building stone by stone;
See him ass-burdened yet without a groan
And look, do, but observe the gorgeous fane
Of yonder lofty Mayan temple, nature bane.
But now, the jungle-smothered ruins proclaim
Proud nature's triumph and of the ancient folk
Only their stone's remain.

This is a lovely land, a fair land, nature's own;
With bush-green valleys and sunsets multi- tone,
Yet the timber cutter sought not nature's ease,
But stood her hardships, her ills without surcease.
He settled not the verdant Stann Creek Valley
Nor Mountain Pine Ridge where one might ever dally,
He chose the field swampy swamp, Old River's estuary
Impelled to it by sheer necessity.
Cast back, dear friend, your eyes to the age past
And see the great logs on the waters cast;
And look, do but observe that splendid slave felling
that magnificent mahogany tree,
Completely free of iron chain on grave.

This is a great land, a good land, nature's place;
Its people free, composed of varied race:
Witness the Carib paddling his canoe,
Or see the Kekchi as he burns anew—
For long and hard our ancestors have worked
In sea and forest where great perils lurked!
Rise up, dear friend, and grasp your neighbour's hand;
With common heart subdue this, nature's land.
In years to come a future generation
Will rise and stand, an independent nation!
And say with pride: "This is our dear land
Given to us by God's and nature's hand."

From *Of Words: An Anthology of Belizean Poetry*, (Cubola Productions: Benque Viejo del Carmen, 1997), pp. 43-44

Base Boy

By Sir Colville Young

Here beside the black waters of the canal
Where the linked turds obscenely float
Here in a decadent old city
We down oceans of raw white rum,
Stupidly drink ourselves to death:
How can death bring worse hell
Than this? Smoke ourselves to hell, snatching
At fugitive glimpses of heaven, bright
Beside the black canals.

How goodly is my heritage
Of brutal slave-holder, and
Of slave-man, slave-woman brutalized
Under the shadow (sub umbra floreo)
Of whip, of gun, of (more terrible
Than bruising of black body) of the washing
Over black soul of sermons at the tides:
"Blessed are the meek for they
Shall inherit the earth" and now
We inherit this rotteness.

The white had his Europe
And the black man his Africa
Till need and greed and history
Brought them together inside me
Under my brown skin. O, Belize,
Heritage bitter as contreebo, bequeathed
By the whip: those who wielded it
And those who felt the weal of it!

Strange how both sufferers thought it,
Stupid and senseless to work;
He with the whip making the other work,
He with reddened black back
Experiencing the profound irony
Of totally unselfish labour
Unselfish because
Nothing of it
Was his.

Two years back, some of us boys
Were exploring the Manhattan sidewalks
Groping numbly, dumbly for better,
Wondering what was better, but certain
We needed it as desperately as thirst
Needs water—and not just money,
Noughts following a number stamped
On paper rectangles or metal circles;
Maybe for pride, respect, and found
No pride, respect in dodging
The immigration authorities.

And as we peeped at each other
Out of long shaggy winter coats
Like hibernating tropical animals
We wondered if that city of so-desired
dollars
 Flowing past like top-gallant floods
Swirling round the glossily labeled food,
The six-packs and candy machines,
The video games and weed joints,
The muggers and the buggers,
The punkies and the junkies,
The fixes and the addicts
And, everlastingly it seemed,
Around us swirling confusion yet clear
The old whiteness and its rightness
With the dollars in its walking
The dollar in its talking,
Could be true—true home.

Till maybe one of the boys said just so
I wonder they doing back home
And the word hurt like a stab-home—
And it's back I come to the open sewers,
To the old canal side base
With a few new vices as sad extra—
For we had been to great Sam, man,
And must show something on return.
Some of us with savings
That trickle away in the new nightclubs
With the razzling, dazzling lights;
Trickle away in base activities:
Gambling, drinking, smoking, showing off,
Cursing politics and politicians,

Soul-talking (dig the crazy jive; cool, man)
Rasta-talking (Jah striking Babylon)
Listening to the strong-bassed Motown sounds
Exploiting the blues that were the cry
Of exploited blackness. Hearing
The angry lament of Tosh and Marley,
The Reggae beat rocking the base
Flowing irresistibly as lava in us
But none of it answering the question
Of what the whole thing is about.

The youngest boy at the base
Got his arm broke last week
When they arrested him and
He resisted. He didn't really mind
The beating (we are used to beatings).
What was harder to take was the station,
Hell away from the more familiar hell;
With the burning throb in his bad arm,
His girl trying to see him and couldn't
And the uniforms asking him over and over
Why this, why that, why the other—
 Why can't you be respectable
Why don't you stop gambling at street corners
Under the lamp-post
Why don't you leave the weed alone
And stop making your fingers fast
With other people's property
Asking over and over again
Maddening, saddening the young boy
With why, why, why and
Nobody knows why.

And here beside the black canals
Her at home at the base
We also wonder why, why
Except for the one—
Who asks when and why not
And he is the terrible one.
Asking why not a cleansing fire
From Vaults to Fort George,
From Belcan to Foreshore—
And he really frightens everybody
Because it's a love—hate feeling we feel
For the decadent old Baymen capital

Won from the swamp inch by inch
With its crowded sing—tables schools
And ramshackle ram-jammed together
Houses with heat-peeled paintlessness
Nakedly pointless where rats and roaches
Compete for the pitiful living space
With our mothers and sisters,
With the little boledo and panades shops
With brave names like Chicago minimarket
And Big Apple saloon, and
We whimper, God Christ, man, you couldn't
Put fire to all that, man,
You must be smoking weed!

But now as time run out
Like the tide in the canal, slow, sluggish
But under the black surface running still,
Some begin to listen, knowing
It wouldn't be Belize in the fire;
Not just Belize cleansed in the fire at last
But a cleansing fire in us,
Inside us all
At the base.

From *From One Caribbean Corner* (National Printers: Belize City, 1993), pp 18-22

Excerpt from Belize, New Nation in Central America

By George C. Price

The Independence of Belize

Belizeans have been struggling for freedom for many years. Our history tells the story of this struggle—of Mayas attacking the colonizers, of slaves rebelling or escaping, of workers striking or rioting, of people demanding their rights.

It was not until the period between the two World Wars however, that a coherent mass movement began to take shape. This movement started out in the town of Belize, but soon spread to other areas of the country. During the 1930's and 1940's, Belizeans openly expressed their new consciousness by participating in mass public meetings and street demonstrations, and by forming mass-based trade unions.

The leaders of the anti-colonial struggle used the Belize City Council, elections to which were subject to a more liberal franchise than the Legislative Assembly, as a platform from which to wage the battle for liberation. In the City Council they expressed their discontent with the colonial government and won the approval of the urban population.

These events unfolded at a time when Belize was experiencing colonial exploitation in the classical manner. Natural resources were extracted from the country and very little was put back. No economic development was talking place; there was considerable poverty and unemployment, social services were inadequate; and communications within the country were primitive. The voice of the people was silenced. All that was needed was a spark to start the fire of the people's political movement.

This spark came with the devaluation of the Belize dollar on December 31, 1949—just a few weeks after the British government had repeatedly given assurances that there would be no devaluation. That night the People's Committee was formed. One of its leaders was George Price. This Committee was later enlarged and became the People's United Party on September 29, 1950. In 1956 George Price became the leader of the party.

The People's United Party was vigorous in its denunciation of colonialism and its demand for self-government.

Among other things, its leaders were charged with sedition, and the forum of their protest, the Belize City Council, was dissolved.

The Party continued its campaign in the face of open hostility from the colonial government. One of its most important demands in those early years was for universal adult suffrage. This was achieved in 1954. Thereafter, the Party spread to the entire country. In a country where the logic of colonialism had created deep divisions between the administrative center and port of Belize City and the rest of the country, it was no easy task the PUP set itself—that of uniting all the people all over the country in a joint effort against colonialism and for self-government. It was a task made even more difficult by the suspicion and distrust that existed between the various ethnic groups as a result of the familiar colonial strategy of divide and rule. But working patiently and hard throughout the years, the Party succeeded in gaining appreciable successes in its fight to unite and build a nation, and within a few years the spirit of nationalism had taken root, in that people from all parts of the country considered themselves a s part of a larger unit, as members of a larger community, and as citizens of a well-organized and functioning state. So successful was the people's movement that in 1961, the British government made it clear that Belize could become constitutionally independent whenever it so desired.

Unfortunately, however, our legitimate aspirations to this independence are being challenged—not, ironically, by the colonizing power, but by a neighboring state which itself had to struggle for its independence from another colonial power, and which as a member of the United Nations should adhere to the principle of the self-determination of peoples.

Guatemalan Claim

Belize has until now been forced not to exercise its inalienable right to independence solely because of the threats of the neighboring country of Guatemala.

Guatemala maintains a claim to the territory of Belize, and has threatened to pursue this claim by force, if necessary. We in Belize, as well as an increasing number of the world's nations, find it difficult to understand the basis of Guatemala's anachronistic claim. Guatemala claims to be the inheritor of Spanish colonialism although Spain never exercised effective jurisdiction over Belize. Guatemala, for her part, admits that she never occupied nor administered the territory of Belize before or after her independence from Spain. Before Guatemala became an independent country, Belize existed as a distinct reality within its present borders.

The Guatemalan claim is in fact precisely what it appears to be—entirely fictitious, unfounded, and unjust. But absurd as this claim is, the threat of a new colonialism represents a frightening reality that is having harsh consequences on the people of Belize.

Under present constitutional arrangements, Britain is responsible for the defense of Belize. When, over a century ago, the Guatemalan claim was being developed, it was the British who conducted negotiations and signed treaties. The Belizean people were not consulted. Since then, the matter has been treated as a dispute between Britain and Guatemala. The British have not yet discharged adequately their responsibility for this problem, and it would be unfair for Belizeans to be left alone to ward off the hostile claims of a country which has a historical dispute with the United Kingdom.

Recognizing this, the People's United Party has declared in its Manifesto for an Independent Belize: "The PUP is determined that the present form of colonialism will not be replaced by colonialism in any other form or from any other source. Likewise, while the PUP is committed to persuade and assist the

United Kingdom government to settle this dispute, the Party's policy remains firm that the sovereignty and independence of Belize is not for negotiation.

"The People's United Party is not prepared to allow this threat indefinitely to postpone the independence of Belize and is prepared to assume the same with any suitable security arrangement that will ensure the safety of the people of Belize and preserve the independence of Belize."

It was the people of Belize who themselves gave birth to the struggle of the peaceful, constructive Belizean revolution to improve the quality of life for all Belizeans and to free Belize from further exploitation by an unjust colonial system. It was the people who first sounded the call for the independence of Belize. And it was out of this desire, and out of their sufferings that a people's movement was born entrusted with the duty to fulfill the people's aspirations.

It is only within the past quarter of a century that the majority of Belizeans have come together to struggle in an organized manner for their liberation. After hundreds of years of exploitation and stagnation, of colonialism and disorganization, the people have come together and created a state—a united people, a vibrant culture, an organized economy, a self-governing entity. Although the successes of the Belizean people has not been complete, their advances are irresistible. There is still much work to be done to rid Belize of all the ill-effects of colonialism. For Belizeans to continue and carry to ultimate success our struggle against colonialism and all its manifestations, we must now take our complete constitutional independence.

From *Belize, A New Nation in Central America* (Cubola Productions: Benque Viejo del Carmen, circa 1960), pp. 36-38

Tears of Freedom

By David Cruz

With straining hearts,
this heavy load
has broken my body and carried me low.
Colonial masters, foreign ideas,
have carried me down and bowed in despair.
How long will I suffer this agony and shame,
This yoke to unburden, and who was to blame?
Who was I, what did I know?
With no place of my own, where could I go?
My colour told me I was part of this land,
I was no Spaniard, American or Englishman.
I longed to reach out
with my brothers to share,
this desire for freedom
and go anywhere.
My heart full of joy, my identity clear,
I'm a Belizean, without any fear.
The date was set, I'm free at last
to unburden my soul and be free of my past.
Twenty-first September of the year '81
I'll always remember as part of the plan
for me to be a citizen free.
I looked to the skies,
wasn't raindrops I felt,
but tears of happiness that came from eyes.

From *Belizean Poets, Part 3* (Belize: Government Printers, circa 1972), p. 36

The Ex-Servicemen's Riot, 1919

The outbreak of World War 1 in 1914 led to a wave of patriotism in British Honduras; request were made in the Colony for the formation of an expeditionary force to supplement The British Expeditionary Forces on the Western Front; in 1915 and 1916 contingents of 129 and 408 respectively left Belize City for the battlefront. Their fate, however, was not to be the glorious one they had anticipated; they were destined for the Rivers Tigris and Euphrates, to work on the Island Water Transport system, and to add insult to injury, they were to be deeply humiliated at the hands of the British soldiery with whom they had come to fight. Samuel Haynes', one of the volunteers, letter to the *Belize Independent* in 1919 gives just a few examples of their treatment:

> Are you aware Mr. Editor that after several attempts on our part to take our stand alongside other British Units on the various battlefields the shocking truth that " it is against a British tradition to employ aboriginal troops against a European enemy" was reluctantly revealed to us?
> On our arrival in Egypt in 1916, our men, hungry and tired, entered he Y.M.C.A. at Gabbary Camp to the strains of 'Rule Britannia.' Imagine our surprise when we were confronted by a number of British soldiers and the question asked 'Who gave you niggers authority to sing that? Clear out of this building—only British troops admitted here.'

By the time the British Honduras contingent returned to the Colony their patriotism had turned to bitterness and resentment; the riot of 1919 was the direct result:

> There was . . . some prior evidence of local dissatisfaction when on 8 July 1919, 339 contingent members returned from Mesopotamia via Taranto in Italy in the *Veronej*. After landing to a decorated capital the men marched to Government House where they were reviewed and addressed by the new Governor, Sir Eyre Houston, who promised them special treatment and provided them all with a meal and $10 each to sustain them until their financial statements were received from Jamaica. After this the men returned to their families and on the next day a social-cum sports was held in their honour. To the authorities this welcome seemed to have taken place very smoothly but even during the celebrations there were indications that some persons were discontented. The Chief Justice afterwards recalled that the contingent members were not specifically invited to tea at the golf club apart from those who came as members' friends. 'On this day they walked up and down in front of the club with their lady friends and saw ladies and gentlemen having tea. One can understand the connection in their minds between this Club and the tummies club in Mesopotamia and the feeling of exclusion connoted.'
> Thirteen days later, on the night of July 22, a section of the contingent, led by one Sergeant Hubert Vernon, moved through the streets of the capital ritually smashing the plate glass windows of the major merchant houses. Combined with this symbolic destruction was a search for certain officials and employers who, on being discovered, were physically assaulted. These assaults

quickly led to mass rioting, the soldiers being joined by 3,000 of the capital's populace in an orgy of looting and destruction which continued well into the morning of the 23rd. The government proved powerless. By 1:00 PM only members of the Territorial Force had answered the bugler's call and it was obvious to the authorities that both the volunteers and the police had sided with the rioters.

A loyal element of the contingent itself and the arrival of *H.M.S Constance* finally subdued the riot.

The incident marked the beginning of black consciousness in the Colony; a consciousness heightened by Marcus Garvey's visit of 1921 and one which was to have lasting influence on subsequent events.[1]

From *The Baymen's Legacy: A Portrait of Belize* (Belize: Cubola Productions, 1987), pp. 57-58

A Si Wha New Belize

By Philip Lewis

A tink a si wha new Belize weh
di Creole man
di Mestizo
di Garifuna
an di Mayan
no separate as a lis dem
but instead all da Belizeans.
"All a wi da wan"
di Creole man sey.
"Todos son hermanos."
Así dice el Mestizo
"Ubafu lun Garifuna."
A wanda weh dende mean?
When Maya man sey "Koten waye."
da ie temple ie wha sho yu.

Who sey me sey Collie Indian no de?
Go da Punta Gorda,
check out Yabra,
di smell da no sere
da tucari an wite rice wid
meat an some good bush.
Climb pan di mule-an-kyart
if ie no wha go, weh di hell
we gwine push it.
Dis ya time da no lakka beffo time,
memba wen we cudn't si?
Now we move di ting fra ova wi eye
an wi get up affa wi knee
All a wi da one a sey
"¿Qué pasa?—yu nho yer mi big
black mout an mi lata brains
man luk ya Bra-da time fi si di
New Belize.

From *Of Words: An anthology of Belizean Poetry* (Cubola Productions: Belize, 1997) p. 29

CONCLUSION

By its very definition, an anthology of any literary genre presupposes that the selected works reflect the bias of the editor and perhaps the publisher. It is my sincere hope that the literary works that have been compiled and chosen for this edition are truly representative of the various Belizean writers. Without question, some important contemporary writers have not been included in this anthology since had they been included then the limited resources available for this literarty endeavor would have been unduly exceeded. Therfore their exclusion in no way reflects negatively on their works of art.

In compiling this anthological edition, I wanted to make available to Belizeans and non-Belizeans alike a compact text, easily accessible and available, which would provide a panoramic representation of the literature of Belize, primarily from the linguistic and cultural perspective. I sincerely hope that this goal has been achieved and as mentioned in the "Acknowledgements," I welcome any academic input from Belizean authors and from Belizeans as well.

NOTES

Introduction

1. A hardwood whose bark was boiled with the resulting liquid being used primarily by the British to dye cloth during the Industrial Revolution.

2. A talking spider who because of his wit, guile and cunning, always seems to get the upper hand in any situation.

Chapter 3

1. Peoples United Party-the political party that has been in power for the longest period of time in the country of Belize. This party led the country to independence in 1981.

2. A. R. Gegg, *British Honduras* (London, 1973), p. 51.

3. C. H. Grant, *The making of modern Belize: Politics, Society and British Colonialism in Central America* (Cambridge, 1976), p. 168.

4. O. Nigel Bolland, *The formation of a colonial society: Belize, from conquest to crown colony* (Baltimore, 1977), p. 25.

5. Cited by Bolland, op. cit. p. 28.

6. Edward Braithwaite and Anthony De V. Phillips, *The people who came, Book 3* (London, 1976), pp. 156-57.

7. H. H. Bancroft, History of Central America, 3 Vols (San Francisco, 1883-87), 2: 626.

8. Captain G. Henderson, *An account of the British settelement at Honduras* (London, 1809), p.59.

9. Superintendent Codd to R. Wilmot, 23 February, 1823, CO 123/124.

10. Frederick Crowe, *The Gospel in Central America*, (London, 1850), p. 33.

11. Crowe, op. cit., 50

12. Sources: 1745, Inhabitants of the Bay of Honduras to Major Caulfield, 18 June 1745, CO 137/148; 1779, unsigned letter to Governor Dalling, 3 September 1779, CO 137/175; 1790a "List of the Inhabitants of Honduras . . . January and February, 1790 . . .." CO 123/11: 1790b "General return of the Inhabitants in the Bay of Honduras . . . 22 October, 1790." CO 123/9;

1803, "A short sketch of the present situation of the Settlement of Honduras" from Superintendent Thomas Barrow, 31 march, 1803, CO 123/15; 1806, Brigadier General H.T. Montresor to Governor Sir Eyre Loote, 22 October, 1806, CO 123/17; 1809, "Remarks upon the situation trade etc." by Barrow, 1st May 1809., CO 123/18; 1816 Census of the population GRB; 1820, Census of the slave population; 31 December, 1820, GRB, 1823, 1826, 1829, 1832 census of the population GRB.

13.   Henderson, op. cit., 75

Chapter 4

1.   A highly prized variety of mango.

2.   Boa-constrictor.

3.   Fer-de-lance, one of the most poisonous snakes of Belize.

Chapter 6

1.   Peter Ashdown, *Race, Class and the Unofficial majority in British Honduras, 1890-1949*, unpublished Ph.D. thesis, University of Sussex, (1979), p. 44.

INDEX

ABOUT THE AUTHOR

Víctor Manuel Durán is a native of the village of Progreso in the north of Belize, Central America. He obtained his Bachelor in Education Degree from McGill University, Montreal, Canada and his graduate degrees from the University of Missouri, Columbia, with emphasis on Latin American Literature, in particular, the contemporary Spanish-American novel and Marxist Literary Theory as it applies to Latin American letters. Currently, he is the Chair of the Department of Languages, Literatures and Cultures at the University of South Carolina Aiken where he also teaches all levels of Spanish language and literature.

www.ingramcontent.com/pod-product-compliance
Lightning Source LLC
Chambersburg PA
CBHW030652110726
47901CB00002B/680